W9-ARW-961

Chicken

GENERAL EDITOR
CHUCK WILLIAMS

RECIPES
EMALEE CHAPMAN

PHOTOGRAPHY
ALLAN ROSENBERG

TIME LIFE BOOKS

Time-Life Books
is a division of TIME LIFE INC.,
a wholly owned subsidary of
THE TIME INC. BOOK COMPANY

President: John M. Fahey

TIME-LIFE BOOKS
President: Mary Davis
Publisher: Robert H. Smith
Vice President and Associate Publisher:
   Trevor Lunn
Vice President and Associate Publisher:
   Susan J. Maruyama
Director of Special Markets: Frances C. Mangan
Marketing Director: Regina Hall
Editorial Director: Lee E. Hassig

WILLIAMS-SONOMA
Founder/Vice-Chairman: Chuck Williams

WELDON OWEN INC.
President: John Owen
Publisher: Wendely Harvey
Managing Editor: Laurie Wertz
Consulting Editor: Norman Kolpas
Copy Editor: Sharon Silva
Editorial Assistant: Janique Poncelet
Design: John Bull, The Book Design Company
Production: Stephanie Sherman, Mick Bagnato
Food Photographer: Allan Rosenberg
Associate Food Photographer: Allen V. Lott
Primary Food & Prop Stylist: Sandra Griswold
Food Stylist: Heidi Gintner
Assistant Food Stylist: Danielle di Salvo
Prop Assistant: Karen Nicks
Glossary Illustrations: Alice Harth

The Williams-Sonoma Kitchen Library
conceived and produced by Weldon Owen Inc.
814 Montgomery St., San Francisco, CA 94133

In collaboration with Williams-Sonoma
100 North Point, San Francisco, CA 94133

Production by Mandarin Offset, Hong Kong
Printed in Hong Kong

A Weldon Owen Production

Copyright © 1993 Weldon Owen Inc.
All rights reserved, including the right of
reproduction in whole or in part in any form.

Library of Congress
Cataloging-in-Publication Data:

Chapman, Emalee.
   Chicken / general editor, Chuck Williams ;
recipes, Emalee Chapman ; photography,
Allan Rosenberg.
      p.   cm. — (Williams-Sonoma
   kitchen library)
   Includes index.
   ISBN 0-7835-0225-7 (trade) ;
   ISBN 0-7835-0226-5 (LSB)
   1. Cookery (Chicken)   I. Williams, Chuck.
II. Title.   III. Series.
TX750.5.C45C43   1993
641.6'65—dc20   92-27836
                                        CIP

Contents

POACHED, BRAISED & STEWED 17

SAUTÉED & FRIED 39

ROASTED & BAKED 65

BROILED & GRILLED 97

INTRODUCTION

"A chicken in every pot" has symbolized widespread prosperity ever since King Henry IV first made such a promise to the citizens of France some four centuries ago.

Today chicken is no longer considered a luxury. Easily prepared, widely available and reasonably priced, it graces tables throughout the world. From whole roast chicken for Sunday dinner to a rapid weeknight stir-fry, from an elegant French-style sauté to fried chicken for the picnic basket, chicken reigns as one of the most versatile main-dish ingredients you can buy.

This book celebrates that versatility. It begins with a guide to the few simple pieces of equipment you'll need to prepare chicken in a multitude of ways, along with information on buying and disjointing chicken, stock making, and basic cooking methods. Following this introductory section are 44 recipes that offer a wide repertoire of chicken dishes, organized into chapters on poaching and stewing, sautéing, roasting and baking, and broiling.

In addition to providing inspiration and good food, I hope this book helps you develop a new sense of economy in the kitchen. Next time you want to sauté or fry chicken pieces, for example, select a whole fresh bird from a quality butcher or poultry shop instead of the prepackaged pieces you might usually buy in a supermarket. Following the simple instructions you'll find here, cut up the chicken yourself. Save trimmings and bones to simmer with an onion, a carrot, some celery, salt and pepper; the simple stock that results will add great flavor to other recipes.

In that spirit, let this book be your guide to putting a chicken in your own pot—as well as in your casserole, frying pan and roasting pan.

EQUIPMENT

Simple, everyday cookware and utensils provide the basics for a vast repertoire of chicken recipes

Chicken's exceptional versatility finds expression in the wide range of equipment shown here. From stockpots to frying pans, casseroles to roasting pans, the array of cooking vessels is as wide ranging as the recipes in this book.

Yet, all the equipment is fairly basic—cookware and utensils any kitchen would do well to have for the preparation of everyday meals. Even the few special tools, such as poultry shears and small boning and carving knives, are not essential to the preparation of a chicken dinner so much as they are aids to make simple work even easier.

1. Pot Holders
Best made of heavy, quilted cotton for good protection from hot cookware, with one side treated for fire resistance.

2. Stockpot
Tall, deep, large-capacity pot with close-fitting lid, for making stock or poaching whole chickens. Select a good-quality, heavy pot that absorbs and transfers heat well. Enameled metal, shown here, cleans easily and does not react with the acidity of any wine, citrus juice or tomatoes that might be used during cooking.

3. Casserole
For oven-baked recipes, available in various sizes and shapes. Choose one with a close-fitting lid, made of good-quality porcelain, stoneware or earthenware.

4. Sauté Pan
For good browning in the early stages of sautéing, select a well-made heavy metal pan large enough to hold chicken pieces in a single layer without crowding. Straight sides help contain splattering. Close-fitting lid covers pan during moist-cooking stage.

5. Kitchen String
For trussing whole chickens before roasting or poaching. Choose good-quality linen string, which withstands an oven's intense, dry heat with minimal charring.

6. Carving Knife and Fork
For easier, neater carving of chicken, select a smaller, more flexible blade and shorter fork than those of the standard carving set commonly used for large roasts.

7. Small Boning Knife
Sharp triangular blade enables easier boning of small chicken pieces. Choose one with a comfortable, well-attached handle.

8. Metal Tongs
Heavy stainless-steel, for turning chicken pieces during cooking. Preferable to a fork, which pierces the meat and releases juices.

10. Wooden Spoons
Wide bowls and sturdy handles allow efficient stirring of casseroles and stews.

11. Skimmer
Wide bowl and fine mesh for efficient removal of froth and scum from surface of chicken stock during its preparation.

12. Chef's Knife
Large, sharp, sturdy knife for cutting up chicken before cooking and for chopping.

13. Boning Knife
Long, slender blade for boning larger pieces.

14. Roasting Pan and Rack
Heavy, durable metal pan, smaller than those used for large roasts; neatly holds a good-sized chicken. Sturdy, hinged metal rack facilitates lifting and turning, promotes more even roasting and prevents chicken from sticking to pan.

15. Cutting Board
Choose one made of tough but resilient white acrylic, which is nonporous and cleans easily. Wood boards, popular in the past, can harbor bacteria and should be avoided for preparation of poultry, meat or seafood, but may be used for vegetables.

16. Rolling Pin
Heavy, dowel-type pin flattens boneless chicken breasts for broiling, grilling, frying or sautéing.

17. Colander
For straining solids from chicken stock.

18. Mixing Bowl
Large capacity for holding colander and containing chicken stock during straining.

19. Poultry Shears
Sharp tapered curved blades—one of them notched to help prevent slipping—easily cut between joints and through bones for disjointing chicken. Select a sturdy, stainless-steel pair.

20. Baking Dish
Select heavy-duty glazed porcelain, stoneware, earthenware or glass for oven-baked chicken recipes, and for holding small chickens for roasting.

21. Measuring Spoons and Cups
For measuring of ingredients. Well-calibrated stainless-steel models with deep bowls provide both durability and accuracy.

22. Bulb Baster
For easy basting of chicken during roasting. Basters with stainless-steel tubes resist heat better than more common plastic models.

23. Basting Brush
For brushing oil, butter or glazes on chicken before or during roasting or broiling. Choose a sturdy, good-sized brush with well-attached natural bristles.

24. Splatter Guard
For placing on top of a frying pan during cooking; fine metal mesh prevents splattering but allows steam to escape.

9. Frying Pan
Choose good-quality, heavy stainless steel, thick aluminum, cast iron or heavy enamel for rapid browning or frying.

Sloped sides facilitate turning of chicken pieces and allow moisture to escape more easily for crisper results.

CHICKEN BASICS

Guidelines to help you select a good-quality, flavorful bird for your dining table

The popularity of chicken has unfortunately led to factory farming that has resulted in the widespread availability of prepackaged birds often lacking distinctive flavor or texture. But good chickens do exist, waiting to be tracked down by dedicated cooks. The best way to find them is to ask questions—of fellow cooks and of local purveyors and chefs. When you taste a good chicken, whether in a restaurant or in someone's home, ask the cook where he or she bought it. Check the Yellow Pages or write the local newspaper's food editor for possible leads on butchers or poulterers that sell fresh, quality birds.

WHAT TO LOOK FOR

First, ask about the source of the chicken and what it was fed on. So-called free-range chickens, allowed to hunt and peck for their varied diet, are likely to be more flavorful. But chickens raised on large-scale, organized breeding farms can also be tasty, provided they were given a good diet of grains.

Choose a chicken with creamy yellow or creamy white skin that looks moist and supple and has well-distributed yellow fat; avoid those that look dried out, discolored, blemished or bruised. Your nose will tell you if a chicken is fresh. If you must buy a prepackaged bird, check the stamped "sell by" date.

A RANGE OF CHOICES

Following are only the main classifications of chicken, and sizes can vary dramatically within each group. For convenience, the recipes in this book call only for broiler-fryer and roasting chickens, but feel free to experiment with the other types.

Broiler-fryer chickens are young, tender birds well suited to broiling and frying, from 2½–4 pounds (1.25–2 kg). Roasting chickens, weighing from 3½–8 pounds (1.75–4 kg) or more, are destined for the oven. Stewing chickens are generally tougher, older birds, weighing from 3–5 pounds (1.5–2.5 kg) or more—good for the slow, moist cooking of the stew pot. Capons are male chickens neutered as chicks, resulting in tender, flavorful roasting birds weighing anywhere from 6–9 pounds (3–4.5 kg). Cornish game hens are a miniature hybrid of chicken weighing no more than 1–2 pounds (500 g–1 kg) and usually cooked by roasting or broiling.

CLEANING, STORING AND FREEZING CHICKEN

As soon as you return from the market, loosen the chicken's wrappings and place it in the coldest part of the refrigerator; bacteria will grow on it at room temperature. Cook the chicken within 2 days. Before cooking, pull out any pin feathers, rinse the chicken with cold water and pat dry with paper towels.

If you wish to keep uncooked chicken longer, freeze it in airtight plastic freezer bags. Thaw in the refrigerator, or place the frozen package in a pan of cold water, changing the water several times. Be sure to allow ample time to defrost completely—as much as 24 hours for a whole roasting bird.

CHICKEN STOCK

Chicken slowly simmered in water with simple seasonings yields a stock that provides the cooking liquid for many stews and braises; moistens quick sautés, casseroles and hashes; and bastes birds as they roast. The chicken meat can be used in salads, casseroles and curries. Stock will keep in a covered container in the refrigerator for up to 5 days, and in the freezer for up to 2 months.

1 chicken, 3–4 lb (1.5–2 kg), or 3 lb (1.5 kg) mixed
    chicken parts
1 lemon, cut in half
1 bay leaf
4 fresh parsley sprigs
2 fresh thyme sprigs
1 celery stalk, cut into pieces
a few peppercorns
sea salt

Place the chicken in a large, deep pot with cold water to cover. Bring slowly to a boil, regularly skimming off any scum and froth that form on the top. Squeeze in a few drops of lemon juice from time to time to keep the stock clear.

Meanwhile, using kitchen string, make a bouquet by tying the bay leaf and parsley and thyme sprigs together. Reduce the heat to low and add the tied herbs, celery and peppercorns to the pot. Cover with the lid slightly ajar and simmer gently for 1½ hours for a whole chicken; smaller, younger chickens or chicken parts should cook only 1 hour. Do not allow the stock to return to a boil or it will become cloudy. Season to taste with salt.

Remove the pot from the heat. Strain the stock into a bowl and let cool. Cover and refrigerate, then lift off the fat that solidifies on top before using.

Makes about 3 qt (3 l)

1. Filling the stockpot.
In a large stockpot, place a whole chicken—3–4 lb (1.5–2 kg)—or an equivalent weight of chicken pieces. Add cold water to cover completely.

2. Skimming the stock.
Bring the liquid slowly to a boil. With a skimmer, regularly skim off the froth and scum from the surface. Add a few drops of lemon juice occasionally to keep the stock clear.

3. Adding the seasonings.
When the stock has reached a gentle boil, reduce the heat to low and add the seasonings. Simmer for 1–1½ hours, skimming as necessary. Take care that the liquid does not return to a boil. Add water as needed to keep chicken covered.

4. Straining the stock.
Remove the stockpot from the heat. Transfer the chicken to a strainer set inside a mixing bowl large enough to hold the liquid. Pour the liquid through the strainer, then lift out the strainer to remove the solids.

5. Removing the fat.
Taste the stock and add salt as needed. Let the stock cool to room temperature, then cover and refrigerate overnight. Using a large spoon, skim off the solidified fat that has risen to the surface of the cooled stock.

CUTTING UP A CHICKEN

Disjointing a chicken yourself saves money—and yields a bonus for the stockpot

The widespread availability today of ready-to-cook chicken pieces has made disjointing—cutting up a whole, uncooked chicken—an endangered art. Yet the techniques involved are fairly simple to master. And a whole chicken will not only cost you significantly less than an equivalent weight of already-cut pieces, but will also yield backbones and other trimmings that can be added to the stockpot.

A sharp, sturdy knife is the only tool you need, or use poultry shears (see pages 6–7). Be sure to work on an acrylic cutting board, which provides a safe, slipproof surface that cleans easily.

Some of the recipes in this book call for quartered or halved chickens, which your butcher or poulterer can prepare for you.

1. Removing the legs.
Place the chicken, breast up and drumsticks toward you, on an acrylic cutting board. With a sharp, sturdy knife, cut through the skin between the thigh and body. Locate the joint by moving the leg, then cut between the thigh and body to remove the leg. Repeat on the other side.

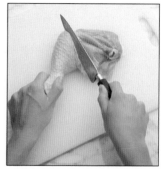

2. Separating the thigh and drumstick.
Move the drumstick to locate the joint connecting it to the thigh. Cut through the joint to separate the two pieces. Repeat with the other leg.

BONING CHICKEN PIECES

A boned chicken breast half provides a neat and elegant portion ideally suited to broiling or sautéing. Stripped of its skin, the breast also makes an excellent low-fat source of protein. Chicken thighs, when boned, produce portions of dark meat ideally suited to quick sautéing and braising.

Start with the breast or thigh portions from a chicken you've already cut up, or with purchased pieces with skin and bones attached. The work goes quickly: one simple step for skinning, and some easy cutting to remove the bones. Be sure to save the bones for the stockpot.

1. Skinning a breast.
Place the breast half, skin-side up, on an acrylic cutting board. Steady the breast meat with the side of a sturdy knife blade or with your hand; with the other hand, firmly grasp the skin and strip it away from the meat.

2. Boning a breast.
Starting along the rib side, insert the knife between the bones and meat. Pressing the knife edge gently against the bones, gradually cut the bones away from the meat. Neatly trim the edges of the breast.

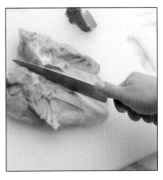

3. Removing the wings.
Move a wing to locate its joint with the body. Cut through the joint to remove the wing. Repeat with the other wing.

4. Cutting off the back.
Starting at the neck opening, cut through both sides of the rib cage, separating the breast section from the remainder of the carcass.

5. Removing the breastbone.
Holding the breast skin-side down, slit the thin membrane covering the breastbone along its center. Grasp the breast firmly at each end and flex it upward to pop out the breastbone. Pull out the bone, using the knife if necessary to help cut it free.

6. Cutting the breast in half.
Place the breast skin-side down on the cutting board. Cut along the center of the breast to split it in half.

Disjointed and neatly trimmed, a whole chicken yields 8 serving-sized pieces ready for cooking: 2 each of thighs, legs, breasts and wings.

3. Boning a thigh.
Remove the skin. Turn the chicken thigh bone-side up. Starting at the wider end of the thigh, use a sharp knife to gradually cut the meat away from the bone, keeping the knife edge against the bone.

POACHING

Making the most of a simple yet versatile cooking method

Gently simmered—or poached—in water, stock or some other flavorful liquid, chicken develops a mild taste and a moist, tender texture that makes it one of the most satisfying ways to enjoy poultry. The resulting stock is a bonus, which can be served as a separate course or used to moisten the sliced chicken meat before serving.

The poaching method shown here may be used as the basis for any number of recipes simply by varying the cooking liquid, filling the chicken's cavity with herbs or aromatic vegetables of your choice, and seasoning to taste. Piquant sauces (see opposite page) may be prepared to lend variety and even more flavor to the delicate cooked chicken. And often, chicken is poached as a preliminary step to another recipe, yielding cooked meat ready to add to a casserole or a salad.

Skinned and boned chicken breasts may be cooked by the same method, using a sauté pan just large and deep enough to hold the breasts side by side and keep them submerged in their poaching liquid. The breasts will be done in no more than 10–15 minutes.

1. Adding flavor enhancements.
For a more attractive presentation, cut off the wing tips. To flavor the chicken subtly while it poaches, fill its cavity with fresh herbs and aromatic vegetables—here, parsley and celery.

2. Trussing the chicken.
To keep the bird compact and neat for serving, you may want to truss it. Cross the drumsticks and tie together with a generous length of kitchen string; tie another length of string around the bird at its wings. Put the chicken in a pot large enough to hold it comfortably.

3. Covering with liquid.
Add enough cold liquid to cover the chicken. Bring to a boil, skimming regularly as shown on page 9. Lower the heat and simmer for 1 hour, skimming as necessary. After 30 minutes, add any sliced vegetable garnishes. Carve as shown on page 15.

SAUCES FOR POACHED CHICKEN

Easily prepared and served alongside freshly poached chicken, any one of the following sauces complements the delicacy of the cooked meat. They'll also perk up leftover chicken that you might wish to serve cold. Make two or more different sauces, offering your guests a choice.

GREEN PARSLEY SAUCE

1 cup (8 fl oz/250 ml) chicken
  stock *(recipe on page 9)*
3 tablespoons chopped fresh parsley
2 tablespoons well-drained capers, coarsely chopped
salt and freshly ground pepper

*P*our the stock into a bowl. Stir in the parsley and capers, mixing well. Season to taste with salt and pepper.

Makes about 1 cup (8 fl oz/250 ml)

HORSERADISH-MUSTARD SAUCE

1 cup (8 fl oz/250 ml) heavy whipping (double)
  cream
1 teaspoon Dijon mustard
2 teaspoons prepared horseradish
1 tablespoon fresh lemon juice
1 tablespoon chopped fresh tarragon
freshly ground pepper

*I*n a bowl whip the cream until stiff peaks form. Using a tablespoon fold in the mustard and horseradish. Stir in the lemon juice and tarragon and season to taste with pepper.

Makes about 1 cup (8 fl oz/250 ml)

RED PEPPER SAUCE

2 red bell peppers (capsicums), seeded,
  deribbed and coarsely chopped
1 clove garlic
1 tablespoon red wine vinegar
½ cup (4 fl oz/125 ml) olive oil
salt and freshly ground pepper

*P*ut the bell peppers in a food processor fitted with the metal blade. Add the garlic and vinegar and process until smooth. Place the purée in a small saucepan over high heat and boil, stirring, until the liquid evaporates, 1–2 minutes. Add the oil and simmer for 1 minute. Season to taste with salt and pepper. Serve at room temperature.

Makes about 1 cup (8 fl oz/250 ml)

TOMATO-CRANBERRY SALSA

2 cups (8 oz/250 g) fresh cranberries
½ cup (4 oz/125 g) coarsely chopped red
  (Spanish) onion
4 tomatoes, coarsely chopped
1 fresh jalapeño pepper, stemmed
2 tablespoons fresh lemon juice
salt

*P*ut the cranberries and onion in a food processor fitted with the metal blade. Chop with off-on pulses. Add the tomatoes and jalapeño pepper and purée. Transfer to a glass or ceramic bowl. Stir in the lemon juice and salt to taste. Allow the flavors to ripen for 1 hour before serving.

Makes about 3 cups (24 fl oz/750 ml)

SAUTÉING

The simple, combined steps of rapid browning and gentle simmering open up a world of culinary variety

The classic cooking method known as sautéing combines the best of two other methods. Like pan frying, it begins by quickly turning or tossing chicken pieces—hence the method's name, from the French *sauter,* "to jump"—in a little hot cooking fat, producing a crisp brown surface that seals in juices.

Then vegetables and liquid can be added to the pan to simmer with the chicken, as in a braised dish or a stew. During this moist-cooking stage, the flavors of the chicken combine with the other ingredients, resulting in tender, tasty meat along with a garnish and a rich sauce.

Beyond these basics, the rest of the process is up to you. Begin with whatever kind of cooking fat you like, whether flavorless vegetable oil or aromatic olive oil; when sautéing with butter, avoid high heat or mix the butter with oil to avoid burning. Whatever your choice, be sure to use just enough to coat the bottom of the pan.

The way you prepare or buy the chicken, too, is a matter of choice. Use basic chicken joints, as shown on pages 10–11, or any combination—all breasts, all thighs, all dark meat or white meat—that suits your taste. Skin or bone the chicken, if you like. Or cut the meat into bite-sized pieces for an Asian-style stir-fry, reducing the cooking time accordingly.

Your selection of vegetable garnishes and cooking liquids, as wide-ranging as the recipes on pages 38–63, will contribute even more variety, suffusing the chicken with their flavors and giving the final dish a unique character.

1. Browning the chicken.
Heat a sauté pan or frying pan over medium heat. Add oil or butter. When it is hot, add the chicken pieces; if the recipe includes garlic, add it now. Cook the chicken until golden brown, about 3 minutes per side, turning with tongs. Carefully pour off all but about 1 tablespoon of fat.

2. Adding vegetables and liquid.
Add any vegetables that the recipe includes—in this case, mushrooms and tomatoes—and sauté in the hot fat, stirring constantly, until they begin to soften, about 2 minutes. Add liquid—usually wine or broth—to the pan, stirring and scraping to dissolve pan deposits.

3. Reducing the sauce.
Add the seasonings, cover the pan, reduce the heat and simmer gently until the chicken is cooked through, about 15 minutes. Remove the chicken. Raise the heat and simmer briskly, stirring continuously, until the liquid thickens and reduces, 2–5 minutes. Adjust the seasonings to taste with salt and pepper.

4. Finishing the dish.
Reduce the heat, return the chicken pieces to the pan, sprinkle with a fresh herb garnish—in this case, chopped parsley—and simmer gently about 2 minutes longer. Serve the chicken immediately, with its vegetables and sauce.

ROASTING

Cooked whole in the intense, dry heat of the oven, a chicken develops crisp, golden brown skin that conceals tender, juicy meat

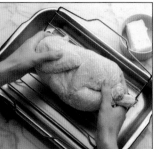

1. Preparing the chicken.
Rinse chicken inside and out; dry with paper towels. Pull out clumps of yellow fat from the cavities at both ends. If you like, rub the inside with a cut lemon. Then rub the inside with 1 tablespoon soft butter or oil. Cut off the wing tips.

2. Trussing the chicken.
Tuck the wings into the body. Pass a 4-foot (120-cm) piece of kitchen string under the chicken at the wing ends, cross the ends over the breast, then cross them again at the tail end. Finally, tie the drumsticks securely, clipping excess string.

3. Buttering the chicken.
Preheat the oven to 400°F (200°C). Coat the chicken generously with oil or softened butter. Place the bird on its side in a roasting pan. Put it into the oven and roast. (Total roasting time is about 20 minutes per · pound/500 g.)

4. Turning and basting.
After 20 minutes, turn the bird onto its other side. Add 2 tablespoons hot water to pan from time to time to keep the chicken moist. Salt the pan juices; baste the bird every 10–15 minutes. After 20 more minutes, turn breast up and reduce the heat to 350°F (180°C).

5. Testing for doneness.
Insert a roasting thermometer into the thickest part of the thigh. It should register 170°–175°F (85°C). Or pierce the thigh (avoiding the bone) with a long fork or skewer; juices should run clear.

6. Carving the chicken.
Transfer to a carving board, breast down, and allow the juices to settle for 5 minutes. Turn breast up. One side at a time, first remove the leg, then separate thigh and drumstick. Slice the breast parallel to the ribs.

STUFFING A ROASTING CHICKEN BENEATH THE SKIN

By inserting seasoned butter between the skin and flesh of a chicken before it is roasted, the bird essentially bastes itself from within, with the butter crisping and browning the skin while it flavors the meat.

Use any combination of fresh or dried herbs, mashing them into softened butter with a table fork. If you like, add a splash of brandy or other flavorful liquid.

With the chicken breast-side up, press down on the breastbone to break and flatten it. Insert your fingers between the skin and flesh, gently separating them. Distribute the butter mixture evenly between skin and flesh.

Chicken Poached with Sausages and Vegetables

1 chicken, about 3½ lb (1.75 kg)
3 carrots, peeled
3 celery stalks, leaves removed
10 small white boiling onions
3 small turnips, peeled
6–8 assorted sausages, 1½–2 lb
  (750 g–1 kg) total weight
salt and freshly ground pepper
2 tablespoons chopped fresh parsley
  for garnish

Serve this simple dish with two sauces: horseradish-mustard sauce and green parsley sauce (recipes on page 13). Use an interesting selection of sausages, such as garlic, veal, turkey and/or chicken. Leave the sausages whole for a stunning presentation, or cut them into thick slices, if you like.

*P*lace the chicken in a large, deep pot and add water to cover. Bring just to a boil over high heat and carefully skim any scum and froth that form on the surface. Reduce the heat to a simmer and add the carrots, celery, onions and turnips. Cover and simmer for 40 minutes.

Add the sausages and simmer, uncovered, until the chicken is tender, about 20 minutes. Season to taste with salt and pepper.

Remove the chicken from the pot and carve it into serving pieces. Arrange the pieces on a large warmed platter. Remove the sausages from the pot and place them around the chicken. Strain the cooking broth, reserving both the broth and vegetables. Arrange the vegetables on the platter. Spoon some of the broth over both the meat and vegetables. Save the remaining broth for another use. Sprinkle the parsley over the chicken and serve.

Serves 6

Chicken Curry

1 chicken, about 3½ lb (1.75 kg)

2 tablespoons unsalted butter

4 green (spring) onions, chopped

3 tablespoons curry powder

1 cup (8 fl oz/250 ml) coconut milk

2 cups (16 fl oz/500 ml) chicken stock
  (recipe on page 9)

3 tablespoons chopped crystallized
  ginger

a few red pepper flakes

2 teaspoons chopped fresh mint or
  1 teaspoon crushed dried mint

2 tablespoons raisins

¼ cup (2 fl oz/60 ml) fresh lime juice

½ cup (4 fl oz/125 ml) heavy
  whipping (double) cream

1 lime, sliced, optional

Create a festive occasion by hosting a curry party. Serve this dish with steamed rice and an assortment of condiments in small ceramic bowls: quartered limes, chutney, chopped cucumber, spiced yogurt, grated coconut, nuts and raisins. Finish the meal with a bowl of chilled fruit ices.

*P*oach the chicken following the basic instructions on page 12. When the chicken is cool, remove the skin and bones. Cut the meat into small cubes and set aside.

Heat the butter in a saucepan over medium heat. Add the onions and sauté until soft, 2–3 minutes. Stir in the curry powder, mixing well with the onions and butter. Gradually add the coconut milk and 1 cup (8 fl oz/250 ml) of the chicken stock and then bring to a boil, stirring to blend well. Reduce the heat and add the ginger, red pepper flakes and mint. Cover and simmer slowly for 30 minutes. Add the reserved chicken pieces and the remaining 1 cup (8 fl oz/250 ml) stock and simmer for 15 minutes. Stir in the raisins, lime juice and cream and simmer for 5 minutes.

Transfer to a warmed serving bowl and garnish with the lime slices, if desired.

Serves 4–6

Paella

1 chicken, about 3½ lb (1.75 kg)

3–4 tablespoons olive oil

1 clove garlic

1 yellow onion, sliced

3 tomatoes, chopped

1 large red bell pepper (capsicum),
   seeded, deribbed and cut into long,
   thin strips

3 cups (24 fl oz/750 ml) chicken stock
   (*recipe on page 9*)

½ cup (4 fl oz/125 ml) dry white wine

½ teaspoon powdered saffron or
   saffron threads

1 cup (6 oz/185 g) Arborio rice

1 cup (4 oz/125 g) shelled green peas

15 large shrimp (prawns) in the shell

12 clams in the shell, well scrubbed

12 mussels in the shell, well scrubbed
   and beards removed

salt and freshly ground pepper

1 lemon, sliced, for garnish

A Spanish classic. Buy clams and mussels with tightly closed shells, and discard any that do not open during cooking. If you like, ½ lb (8 oz/250 g) lobster tail—shelled and cut into slices ½ inch (12 mm) thick—can be added with the shrimp.

Cut the chicken into 8 pieces as directed on pages 10–11. Trim off any excess fat.

Warm the oil in a broad, deep frying pan over medium-high heat. Add the garlic and chicken and sauté, turning the pieces as they become golden, 3–4 minutes on each side. Remove the garlic and discard. Transfer the chicken to a plate and set aside. Reduce the heat and stir in the onion, tomatoes and bell pepper. Sauté for 2–3 minutes.

In a bowl combine the chicken stock and wine and add the saffron. Let stand for a few minutes and then add to the pan. Bring to a boil and add the rice. Reduce the heat to low, return the chicken to the pan and simmer gently for 15 minutes.

When the rice is plump and half cooked, add the peas, shrimp, clams and mussels and simmer for 5 minutes. Season to taste with salt and pepper and cook until the rice is completely tender, about 5 minutes longer. Transfer the paella to a large warmed platter, with the rice surrounding the chicken and shellfish. As the paella is served, place a slice of lemon on each plate.

Serves 4–6

Chicken Stuffed with Herbs and Cheese

2 tablespoons chopped fresh parsley
1 tablespoon chopped fresh thyme or
   1 teaspoon dried thyme
1 tablespoon chopped fresh chives
¼ cup (1 oz/30 g) freshly grated
   Parmesan cheese
5 tablespoons (2½ fl oz/80 ml) olive
   oil
8 chicken thighs
1 cup (8 fl oz/250 ml) chicken stock
   (recipe on page 9)
½ cup (4 fl oz/125 ml) dry white wine
2 carrots, peeled and sliced
1 yellow onion, sliced
2 leeks, white part only, trimmed,
   carefully washed and sliced
salt and freshly ground pepper
fresh herb sprigs for garnish

As the chicken cooks, a lovely sauce forms in the pan. Serve warm country-style bread to mop up the delicious juices.

In a small bowl stir together the parsley, thyme, chives, Parmesan cheese and 2 tablespoons of the oil.

Skin and bone the chicken thighs as directed on pages 10–11. Trim off any excess fat. Slit the underside of each thigh, if necessary, so the meat lies flat; lay underside up. Place 1 tablespoon of the herb mixture on the center of each thigh and fold in the sides to enclose it. Secure each thigh with 2 toothpicks.

Warm the remaining 3 tablespoons oil in a large sauté pan over medium heat. Add the thighs, seam side down, and sauté, turning them as they become golden, 3–4 minutes on each side. Remove and set aside.

Pour the stock into the pan and bring to a boil over high heat. Deglaze the pan by stirring to dislodge any browned bits. Reduce the heat and add the wine, carrots, onion and leeks. Return the chicken to the pan and season to taste with salt and pepper. Cover and simmer until the chicken and vegetables are tender when pierced, about 30 minutes.

Place the vegetables and sauce on a warmed platter. Arrange the chicken on top. Garnish with herb sprigs.

Serves 4–6

Spanish Chicken

1 chicken, about 3½ lb (1.75 kg), or
   8–10 chicken legs
¼ cup (2 fl oz/60 ml) olive oil
2 cloves garlic, cut in half
4 slices boiled ham, cut lengthwise
   into strips ½ inch (12 mm) wide
1 small onion, chopped
1 small red bell pepper (capsicum),
   seeded, deribbed and chopped
¼ teaspoon red pepper flakes
1 cup (8 fl oz/250 ml) chicken stock
   (recipe on page 9)
2 tomatoes, sliced
½ cup (4 fl oz/125 ml) dry sherry
salt and freshly ground pepper

A colorful blend of tastes and flavors that capture the festive spirit of Spain: red peppers, sherry and ham. Garnish with asparagus tips and parsley, and serve with saffron rice and a green salad tossed with sherry vinaigrette.

*I*f using a whole chicken, cut into 8 pieces as directed on pages 10–11. Trim off any excess fat.

Warm the oil in a large sauté pan over medium heat. Add the garlic and sauté until brown, 2–3 minutes. Remove the garlic and discard.

Add the chicken pieces and sauté, turning as they become golden, 3–4 minutes on each side. Remove from the pan and set aside. Add the ham and stir for 2–3 minutes. Add the onion and bell pepper and sauté until soft, 4–5 minutes. Mix in the red pepper flakes.

Add ½ cup (4 fl oz/125 ml) of the chicken stock to the pan and bring to a boil over high heat. Deglaze the pan by stirring to dislodge any browned bits; boil for 2–3 minutes. Add the remaining ½ cup (4 fl oz/125 ml) stock. Reduce the heat to a simmer, add the tomatoes and cook for 5 minutes.

Return the chicken to the pan, stir in the sherry and season to taste with salt and pepper. Cover and simmer until tender, 30–40 minutes.

Transfer the chicken and the sauce to a warmed serving dish.

Serves 4

Malaysian Chicken Breasts with Endive and Ginger

2 whole chicken breasts
4 cups (32 fl oz/1 l) chicken stock
  (recipe on page 9)
1 small piece fresh ginger, peeled and
  cut crosswise into 4 thin slices
1 bay leaf
2 celery hearts, thinly sliced
4 green (spring) onions, cut into thin
  strips on the diagonal
2 heads Belgian endive (chicory/
  witloof), cut into quarters lengthwise
salt and freshly ground pepper
2 tablespoons chopped fresh chives
  for garnish

The subtle flavors of Malaysia are found in this pretty green-and-white chicken dish. Serve with wild rice mixed with golden raisins and toasted hazelnuts (filberts).

*H*alve, skin and bone the chicken breasts as directed on pages 10–11. Trim off any excess fat and set the breasts aside.

Pour the stock into a saucepan and place over medium heat. Bring to a boil, reduce the heat and simmer for 2 minutes to concentrate the flavor. Cut the ginger slices into thin strips and add them to the pan with the bay leaf and celery hearts. Simmer for 5 minutes.

Add the chicken breasts, green onions and endives and cook until the chicken is tender, 10–12 minutes. The vegetables should remain green. Season to taste with salt and pepper.

Place each chicken breast half in an individual bowl. Divide the ginger and vegetables among the bowls and add a few tablespoons of the cooking broth. Garnish with the chives.

Serves 4

Paprika Chicken

8 chicken legs
8 chicken thighs
2 lemons
2 tablespoons unsalted butter
2 tablespoons olive oil
1 yellow onion, chopped
2 tablespoons Hungarian paprika
a few grains cayenne pepper
½ cup (4 fl oz/125 ml) chicken stock
    (*recipe on page 9*)
2 tomatoes, chopped
½ cup (4 fl oz/125 ml) heavy
    whipping (double) cream
salt and freshly ground pepper

The Ottoman Turks, who carried back spices from their far-flung conquests, introduced this rich dish to Eastern Europe. Serve with noodles tossed with sesame seeds, and an apple and watercress salad.

Remove the skin from the chicken pieces, if desired, and then trim off any excess fat. Place the chicken in a single layer in a bowl and squeeze the juice of ½ lemon evenly over the top.

Warm the butter and oil in a large sauté pan over medium heat. Add the chicken pieces and sauté, turning them as they become golden, 3–4 minutes on each side. Stir in the onion and sauté until soft, 2–3 minutes. Mix in the paprika and cayenne pepper. Add the stock and bring to a boil for a few seconds over high heat. Deglaze the pan by stirring to dislodge any browned bits. Reduce the heat to low, cover and simmer for 20 minutes.

Meanwhile, in a small saucepan over medium heat, cook the tomatoes until soft and the liquid evaporates, 3–4 minutes. Force them through a sieve with a wooden spoon, then add to the chicken. Cook for 10 minutes longer.

Transfer the chicken to a warmed platter. Stir the cream into the pan juices and heat thoroughly. Add the juice of the remaining ½ lemon and season to taste with salt and pepper. Pour over the chicken. Cut the remaining lemon into quarters and serve with the chicken.

Serves 4–6

Chicken with Spring Vegetables

1 chicken, about 3½ lb (1.75 kg)

3 tablespoons unsalted butter

1 shallot, finely chopped

¼ cup (2 fl oz/60 ml) white wine

½ cup (4 fl oz/125 ml) chicken stock
  (recipe on page 9)

1 tomato, peeled and sliced

salt and freshly ground pepper

1 cup (4 oz/125 g) shelled green peas

8 small white boiling onions

2 fresh thyme sprigs

½ cup (4 oz/125 g) chopped carrot

4 lettuce leaves

½ cup (4 fl oz/125 ml) water

shavings of Parmesan cheese for
  garnish

Make this dish in springtime when the vegetables are young and tender. Using a vegetable peeler, cut curls of Parmesan cheese for garnish. Pasta tossed with red pepper sauce (recipe on page 13) makes a nice accompaniment.

Cut the chicken into 8 pieces as directed on pages 10–11. Trim off any excess fat.

Melt the butter in a sauté pan over medium heat. Add the chicken and sauté, turning the pieces as they become golden, 3–4 minutes on each side. Cover with the lid slightly ajar and cook gently for 3–4 minutes. Remove the chicken and set aside.

Stir the shallot into the pan, then pour in the wine and stock and add the tomato. Stir well and cook for 5 minutes; season to taste with salt and pepper. Return the chicken to the pan. Cover and simmer for 20 minutes.

Meanwhile, in a saucepan combine the peas, onions, thyme, carrot, lettuce leaves and water. Cover and simmer over low heat until the vegetables are tender, about 6 minutes. Drain the vegetables, reserving the liquid. Add the vegetables to the pan holding the chicken and simmer gently for 5 minutes. Add 2 tablespoons of the reserved liquid if the vegetables begin to stick.

Transfer the chicken pieces and vegetables to a warmed platter. Garnish with the Parmesan cheese.

Serves 4 or 5

Mediterranean Chicken

1 chicken, about 3½ lb (1.75 kg)

1 tablespoon dried basil

2 tablespoons olive oil

1 clove garlic, cut in half

1 red bell pepper (capsicum), seeded, deribbed and chopped

grated zest of 1 orange

¼ cup (2 fl oz/60 ml) chicken stock (*recipe on page 9*)

salt and freshly ground pepper

½ cup (3 oz/90 g) thinly sliced fennel

¼ cup (2 fl oz/60 ml) dry white wine

16 small black olives, preferably Greek or Italian

An interesting mix of aromatic flavors reminiscent of the warm Mediterranean sun: basil, garlic, zest of orange, olives and fennel. Serve with room-temperature broccoli or green beans vinaigrette, as the Latins do.

Cut the chicken into 8 pieces as directed on pages 10–11. Trim off any excess fat; sprinkle the chicken with the basil.

Warm the oil in a sauté pan over medium heat. Add the garlic and chicken and sauté, turning the pieces as they become golden, 3–4 minutes on each side. Remove the garlic and discard. Add the bell pepper and orange zest and cook for 2 minutes.

Stir in the chicken stock and season to taste with salt and pepper; mix in the fennel. Add the white wine, cover and simmer gently until the chicken is tender, 30–40 minutes. During the last 10 minutes of cooking, uncover the pan and mix in the olives.

Transfer the chicken to a warmed platter and surround with the vegetables and pan juices.

Serves 4

Chicken Stew with Parsley Dumplings

4 chicken legs
4 chicken thighs
6 cups (48 fl oz/1.5 l) chicken stock
  (*recipe on page 9*)
3 celery stalks
4 small turnips, peeled
4 carrots, peeled
2 russet potatoes, peeled
2 leeks, white part only, trimmed and
  carefully washed
1 tomato
salt and freshly ground pepper

FOR THE DUMPLINGS:
1 egg
2 tablespoons water
salt
dash of paprika
a few grains cayenne pepper
1 teaspoon unsalted butter, melted
¾ cup (3 oz/90 g) all-purpose (plain)
  flour
1 teaspoon baking powder
3 tablespoons finely chopped fresh
  parsley

A hearty and satisfying stew for a cold winter day.

Place the chicken pieces in a deep, heavy pot and add the stock. Bring to a boil over high heat, then reduce the heat to a simmer. Skim any froth and scum that form on the surface. Coarsely chop the celery, turnips, carrots, potatoes, leeks and tomato and add them to the pot. Simmer gently for 15 minutes, then season with salt and pepper. Lift out the vegetables with a slotted spoon and place in a food processor fitted with the metal blade. Process to form a thick purée. Stir the purée into the pot with the chicken and simmer for 10 minutes while making the dumplings.

In a bowl stir together the egg, water, salt to taste, paprika, cayenne and melted butter. In another bowl mix together the flour and baking powder, then stir into the egg mixture to form a thick, smooth batter. Stir in 2 tablespoons of the parsley.

Using a teaspoon, drop the batter by spoonfuls into the simmering stew. Cover the pot and simmer without raising the lid for 15 minutes. Lift out a dumpling and test to see if it is cooked. If it is still floury, re-cover the pot and cook 3–4 minutes longer.

Transfer the chicken, dumplings and vegetable purée to a deep platter. Sprinkle with the remaining 1 tablespoon parsley and serve.

Serves 4

Basque Chicken

1 chicken, about 3½ lb (1.75 kg)

3 tablespoons olive oil

½ teaspoon dried thyme

½ teaspoon dried oregano

2 shallots, chopped

2 tomatoes, sliced

1 cup (8 fl oz/250 ml) chicken stock
   (*recipe on page 9*)

salt and freshly ground pepper

½ cup (2½ oz/75 g) green olives,
   preferably Italian

½ cup (2½ oz/75 g) black olives,
   preferably Italian

A lovely dish for early autumn when ripe red tomatoes are still on the vine. The tomatoes and olives impart a rich quality to the chicken. A large mound of polenta is a delicious accompaniment to the sauce. Serve fall pears cooked in white wine for dessert.

Skin the chicken and cut into 8 pieces as directed on pages 10–11. Trim off any excess fat.

Warm the oil in a large sauté pan over medium heat. Stir in the thyme and oregano and add the chicken. Sauté, turning the pieces as they become golden, 3–4 minutes on each side.

Add the shallots and tomatoes and stir until soft, 2–3 minutes. Pour in ½ cup (4 fl oz/125 ml) of the stock and bring to a boil. Deglaze the pan by stirring to dislodge any browned bits. Season to taste with salt and pepper. Add the green and black olives, reduce the heat to low, cover and simmer gently for 30 minutes.

Stir the sauce and then pour in the remaining ½ cup (4 fl oz/125 ml) stock. Simmer until the chicken is tender, about 15 minutes.

Transfer the chicken to a warmed platter with the sauce and serve.

Serves 4

Fried Chicken with Herbs

2 chickens, about 2½ lb (1.25 kg)
   each
1 cup (4 oz/125 g) all-purpose (plain)
   flour
salt
1 teaspoon paprika
1 teaspoon dried thyme
1 teaspoon dried sage
10 fresh parsley sprigs
about 2 cups (16 fl oz/500 ml)
   vegetable oil or peanut oil
2 lemons, cut into quarters, for
   garnish

Pack this crisp chicken for a picnic, or accompany it with corn on the cob, a tossed vegetable salad, or a cold soup. Serve the chicken with red pepper sauce and tomato-cranberry salsa (recipes on page 13).

Cut each chicken into 8 pieces as directed on pages 10–11. Trim off any excess fat.

In a sturdy paper bag, combine the flour, salt to taste, paprika, thyme and sage; shake well to blend thoroughly. Add the chicken pieces to the bag, 3 or 4 at a time, and shake to coat. Shake off the excess and set aside. Add the parsley sprigs to the flour mixture and shake to coat. Remove the parsley sprigs and set aside.

Pour the oil into a deep, heavy saucepan to a depth of 1½ inches (4 cm). Place over medium heat until the oil is very hot (350°F/180°C). When the oil is ready, slip 3 of the chicken pieces into the pan. Do not crowd the pan or the chicken will not brown evenly. Cook over medium-high heat, turning to brown on all sides, until golden brown, about 3 minutes. Reduce the heat to low and cook through, 4–5 minutes. Transfer to paper towels to drain. Place the chicken in a warm oven. Repeat with the remaining chicken pieces.

Add the parsley sprigs to the hot oil and fry until golden, 1–2 minutes. Transfer to paper towels to drain.

Place the chicken pieces on a warmed platter. Garnish with the fried parsley and lemon quarters.

Serves 4–6

Saffron Chicken with Capers

2 whole chicken breasts

2 tablespoons unsalted butter

2 cloves garlic, cut in half

green tops of 4 green (spring) onions, slivered lengthwise and then cut crosswise into ½-inch (12-mm) pieces

½ cup (4 fl oz/125 ml) dry white wine

½ teaspoon powdered saffron or saffron threads

salt and freshly ground pepper

¼ cup (2 oz/60 g) well-drained capers

A light spring or summer dish. The saffron and capers provide a unique blend of flavors. Serve with young carrots, slender string beans or grilled tomato halves.

Halve, skin and bone the chicken breasts as directed on pages 10–11, then cut each half-breast in half lengthwise. Trim off any excess fat.

Melt the butter in a sauté pan over medium heat. Add the garlic and sauté until soft, 1–2 minutes. Add the chicken pieces and sauté on each side for 2 minutes; do not brown. Remove the garlic and discard. Remove the chicken and set aside.

Add the green onions to the pan and sauté in the butter for 1 minute. Combine the wine and saffron, stir the mixture into the pan and simmer for 2 minutes. Return the chicken to the pan and cook until tender, about 5 minutes. Season to taste with salt and pepper. Place the chicken breasts on a warmed platter. Pour the sauce over the chicken and sprinkle with the capers.

Serves 4

Chicken Paillard

2 chicken thighs
1 whole chicken breast
¼ cup (2 oz/60 g) unsalted butter, melted
1 teaspoon dried sage
1 teaspoon dried thyme
salt and freshly ground pepper

If possible use a cast-iron frying pan for this recipe, which cooks the chicken over high heat. Serve with crisp thin potatoes, skewers of grilled vegetables, and a salad of watercress and Belgian endive (chicory/witloof) tossed with herb vinaigrette. Offer horseradish-mustard sauce (recipe on page 13) on the side.

Skin and bone the thighs as directed on pages 10–11; trim off any excess fat. Slit the underside of each thigh, if necessary, so that the meat lies flat. Place the thighs between 2 sheets of waxed paper and, using a rolling pin, flatten until the meat is of an even thickness, about ⅛ inch (3 mm).

Halve, skin and bone the breasts as directed on pages 10–11. Trim off any excess fat. Place the breasts between 2 sheets of waxed paper and, using a rolling pin, flatten them in the same manner.

Brush each chicken piece on both sides with the melted butter and then sprinkle with the sage and thyme.

Heat a heavy frying pan over high heat until very hot. Add the chicken and cook quickly, 1–2 minutes on each side. Season to taste with salt and pepper, transfer to a warmed platter and serve at once.

Serves 2–4

Chicken with Apples

2 whole chicken breasts
¼ cup (2 oz/60 g) unsalted butter
1 teaspoon dried thyme
3 green apples, cored and thickly
  sliced crosswise
2 tablespoons sugar
3 tablespoons Calvados or brandy
½ cup (4 fl oz/125 ml) apple juice
2 leeks, white part only, trimmed,
  carefully washed and chopped
½ cup (4 fl oz/125 ml) heavy
  whipping (double) cream
salt and freshly ground pepper

A satisfying cold-weather dish. Calvados, an apple brandy from Normandy, imparts a special flavor to the chicken.

*H*alve, skin and bone the chicken breasts as directed on pages 10–11. Trim off any excess fat.

Melt the butter in a large sauté pan over medium heat. Stir in the thyme and add the chicken pieces. Sauté, turning the pieces as they become golden, 3–4 minutes on each side. Add the apple slices and cook, turning once, until soft, 3–4 minutes. Transfer the apples to a plate and sprinkle with the sugar.

Pour off the oil from the chicken. Pour the Calvados or brandy into a small saucepan and warm gently. Using a long-handled match, ignite the liquor. When the flame dies, pour the liquor over the chicken. Add the apple juice and arrange the leeks around the chicken. Cover and cook over medium-low heat until the chicken is tender, about 15 minutes.

Using a slotted spoon, transfer the chicken and leeks to a warmed platter, leaving the ends of the platter uncovered.

Pour the cream into the pan and bring to a boil over high heat. Deglaze the pan by stirring to dislodge any browned bits. Boil to thicken the sauce slightly, about 2 minutes. Season to taste with salt and pepper.

Pour the sauce over the chicken. Place the apple rings on the ends of the platter.

Serves 4

Chicken with Artichokes

1 chicken, about 3½ lb (1.75 kg)

1 tablespoon dried marjoram

3 tablespoons unsalted butter

2 shallots, chopped

2 tablespoons chopped fresh parsley

½ cup (4 fl oz/125 ml) chicken stock
    (recipe on page 9)

6 frozen artichoke hearts, thawed and
    thickly sliced lengthwise

¼ cup (2 fl oz/60 ml) sweet vermouth

salt and freshly ground pepper

½–¾ cup (4–6 fl oz/125–180 ml)
    heavy whipping (double) cream

When baby artichokes are in season and very tender, use them in place of frozen hearts: Cut off the prickly top halves and discard, then thinly slice the bottom halves. The mix of artichokes, cream and chicken makes this a glorious dish. Serve with roasted new potatoes.

Cut the chicken into 8 pieces as directed on pages 10–11. Remove the skin and excess fat. Sprinkle the chicken with the marjoram.

Melt the butter in a large sauté pan over medium heat. Add the chicken and sauté, turning the pieces as they become golden, 3–4 minutes on each side. Remove and set aside.

Stir in the shallots and 1 tablespoon of the parsley and sauté until the shallots are soft but not brown, 1–2 minutes. Add the chicken stock and bring to a boil. Deglaze the pan by stirring to dislodge any browned bits. Add the artichoke hearts and return the chicken to the pan. Reduce the heat to low and cook for 10 minutes.

Add the vermouth and season to taste with salt and pepper. Simmer uncovered for 5 minutes. Pour in the cream and simmer, stirring while the sauce thickens, for 5 minutes. Transfer to a warmed platter and sprinkle with the remaining 1 tablespoon parsley.

Serves 3 or 4

Chicken Salad with Radicchio and Red Onions

2 whole chicken breasts

½ cup (2 oz/60 g) all-purpose (plain) flour

2 eggs

salt and freshly ground pepper

½ cup (2 oz/60 g) freshly grated Parmesan or Romano cheese

1 cup (8 fl oz/250 ml) sesame oil or safflower oil

1 small head radicchio (red chicory), thinly sliced lengthwise

1 small bunch arugula (rocket), separated into leaves

1 red (Spanish) onion, thinly sliced

½ cup (4 fl oz/125 ml) olive oil

¼ cup (2 fl oz/60 ml) balsamic vinegar

2 tablespoons fresh lemon juice

Here is a light main dish that goes well with corn bread and strawberries glazed with sugar.

Halve, skin and bone the chicken breasts as directed on pages 10–11. Trim off any excess fat. Place the breasts between 2 sheets of waxed paper and, using a rolling pin, flatten until the meat is of an even thickness, about ¼ inch (6 mm). Lightly dust each breast with flour and shake off the excess. In a bowl beat together the eggs and salt and pepper to taste. Dip the chicken pieces into the egg mixture to coat both sides thoroughly. Then dip into the cheese to coat.

Warm the sesame or safflower oil in a heavy frying pan over medium heat. When the oil is hot, add 2 breast halves and cook, turning as they become golden brown, 1–2 minutes on each side. Transfer to paper towels to drain. Repeat with the remaining 2 breast halves.

In a large bowl combine the radicchio, arugula and onion, reserving a few onion slices for garnish.

In a small bowl whisk together the olive oil, vinegar and lemon juice; season to taste with salt and pepper. Pour over the salad greens and toss well.

Slice each chicken breast lengthwise into thin strips. Place the salad greens on a large serving plate. Top with the chicken strips and remaining onion slices.

Serves 4

Mexican Chicken with Salsa

Served on a bed of lettuce and accompanied with corn tortillas, this marvelous Mexican-inspired dish is good fare for a warm summer day—or anytime.

FOR THE SALSA:

1 small avocado, peeled, pitted and
   coarsely chopped
juice of 1 lime
1 small tomato, coarsely chopped
2 tablespoons sesame oil
½ cup (4 oz/125 g) chopped red
   (Spanish) onion
2 tablespoons chopped fresh cilantro
   (fresh coriander)
salt and red pepper flakes

2 whole chicken breasts
2 limes
2 tablespoons sesame oil
2 cloves garlic, cut in half
½ cup (4 fl oz/125 ml) chicken stock
   (*recipe on page 9*)
salt and red pepper flakes
1 head green leaf lettuce, separated
   into leaves and sliced into long, thin
   strips
4 fresh cilantro (fresh coriander) sprigs
   for garnish
8 corn tortillas, warmed

*T*o make the salsa: In a bowl combine the avocado, lime juice, tomato, oil, onion, cilantro and salt and pepper flakes to taste. Stir to mix well and set aside.

Halve, skin and bone the chicken breasts as directed on pages 10–11. Trim off any excess fat. Cut lengthwise into strips 1 inch (2.5 cm) wide and place in a bowl. Squeeze the juice of 1 lime over the chicken and toss gently.

Warm the oil in a large sauté pan over medium heat. Add the garlic and sauté until soft, 1–2 minutes. Discard the garlic. Add the chicken and sauté, turning the pieces as they become golden, about 1 minute on each side. Transfer to a warmed plate; keep warm. Pour off the oil from the pan. Add the chicken stock to the pan and bring to a boil over high heat. Deglaze the pan by stirring to dislodge any browned bits. Reduce the liquid by about one half. Season with salt and pepper flakes.

Arrange some lettuce on individual plates and top with some of the chicken strips. Pour the warm sauce over the chicken, then add some salsa to each plate. Cut the remaining lime into quarters. Garnish each plate with a lime quarter and a cilantro sprig. Serve with a basket of warmed tortillas.

Serves 4

Chicken Breasts with Vermouth

2 whole chicken breasts
¼ cup (1 oz/30 g) all-purpose (plain)
  flour
1 teaspoon dried sage
3 tablespoons unsalted butter
½ cup (4 fl oz/125 ml) dry vermouth
1 tablespoon fresh lemon juice
salt and freshly ground pepper
zest of 1 lemon
4 fresh basil leaves for garnish,
  optional

A light, quick and easy chicken dish. Good with a Belgian endive (chicory/witloof) and fennel salad, and in springtime with fresh asparagus tips. Noodles with fresh basil and butter also make a delicious accompaniment.

*H*alve, skin and bone the chicken breasts as directed on pages 10–11. Trim off any excess fat. Place the breasts between 2 sheets of waxed paper and, using a rolling pin, flatten them slightly and evenly. Mix the flour and sage together. Dust the breasts lightly with the flour mixture, then shake off the excess.

Melt the butter in a sauté pan over medium heat. Add the chicken breasts and sauté, turning as they become golden, 2–3 minutes on each side. Transfer to a warmed platter; keep warm.

Pour the vermouth into the pan and bring to a boil over high heat. Deglaze the pan by stirring to dislodge any browned bits; boil until the sauce is reduced by one half, 2–3 minutes. Add the lemon juice and season to taste with salt and pepper.

Pour the sauce over the chicken breasts, sprinkle with the zest and garnish with the basil, if desired.

Serves 4

Stir-Fry Chicken with Vegetables

1 chicken, about 3½ lb (1.75 kg)

3 tablespoons sesame oil

2 slices fresh ginger

2 cloves garlic, cut in half lengthwise

½ cup (2 oz/60 g) sliced fresh mushrooms

½ cup (4 oz/125 g) sliced celery

½ cup (3 oz/90 g) green beans, cut crosswise into 1-inch (2.5-cm) lengths

¼ cup (2 fl oz/60 ml) chicken stock (recipe on page 9)

4 tablespoons chopped fresh cilantro (fresh coriander)

¼ cup (1 oz/30 g) sliced almonds

salt and freshly ground white pepper

fresh cilantro (fresh coriander) for garnish

This chicken stir-fry abounds with fresh vegetables. Complete the dish with steamed rice.

❦

Cut the chicken into 8 pieces as directed on pages 10–11. Skin the pieces and cut the meat from the bones in large pieces. Trim off any excess fat. Place the pieces between 2 sheets of waxed paper and, using a rolling pin, flatten them slightly and evenly. Cut into long strips about ½ inch (12 mm) wide.

Warm 2 tablespoons of the oil in a large sauté pan or wok over medium heat. Add the ginger and stir for 1 minute. Add the chicken strips and stir-fry until golden, 1–2 minutes on each side. Remove the chicken and set aside. Discard the ginger.

Add the remaining 1 tablespoon oil to the pan and stir in the garlic, mushrooms, celery and beans. Stir-fry for 1–2 minutes over medium heat. Add the chicken stock and cook over medium-high heat until the vegetables just begin to soften, 4–5 minutes. Discard the garlic.

Reduce the heat to low and stir in the chopped cilantro and almonds. Return the chicken to the pan and stir-fry with the vegetables until heated through and the vegetables are tender, 3–4 minutes. Season to taste with salt and white pepper.

Transfer to a warmed platter; garnish with the cilantro.

Serves 4–6

Chicken Breasts, Italian Style

2 whole chicken breasts
2 eggs
1 teaspoon salt
2 tablespoons water
2 tablespoons all-purpose (plain) flour
½ cup (2 oz/60 g) dried bread crumbs
½ cup (4 fl oz/125 ml) vegetable oil
freshly ground pepper
2 lemons, cut in half
2 tablespoons well-drained capers,
   optional

Chicken breasts cooked in this manner are a light main course. Green peas add the final touch. Place a bowl of green parsley sauce (recipe on page 13) on the table.

Halve, skin and bone the chicken breasts as directed on pages 10–11. Trim off any excess fat. Place the breasts between 2 sheets of waxed paper and, using a rolling pin, flatten until the meat is of an even thickness, about ½ inch (12 mm). Trim the meat into uniform ovals.

In a bowl beat the eggs with the salt and water. Dip the chicken breasts, one at a time, into the egg mixture. Dust each breast lightly with flour and then roll in the bread crumbs to coat.

Warm the oil in a deep, heavy frying pan over medium heat. Place the breasts in the hot oil and fry, turning as they become golden, 3–4 minutes on each side. Transfer to paper towels to drain. Season to taste with pepper.

Serve on warmed plates with a lemon half and 1½ teaspoon capers, if you like, on each breast.

Serves 4

Creamed Chicken

4 tablespoons (2 oz/60 g) unsalted
  butter
½ cup (4 oz/125 g) finely chopped red
  or yellow bell pepper (capsicum)
½ cup (4 oz/125 g) chopped shallots
2 tablespoons chopped fresh parsley
2 tablespoons all-purpose (plain) flour
2½ cups (20 fl oz/625 ml) chicken
  stock, heated (recipe on page 9)
¼ teaspoon paprika
⅛ teaspoon cayenne pepper
salt and freshly ground pepper
½ cup (4 fl oz/125 ml) heavy
  whipping (double) cream
2 cups (12 oz/375 g) chopped, cooked
  chicken

Use poached chicken meat (see method on page 12) for making this old favorite. Serve it with tomato-cranberry salsa (page 13), along with baked potatoes and halved tomatoes that have been brushed with vinaigrette and put under the broiler for a few minutes. Fresh fruit provides a nice finish.

Melt 2 tablespoons of the butter in a sauté pan over medium heat. Add the bell pepper and sauté for 1 minute. Add the shallots and sauté until soft, 3–4 minutes. Stir in 1 tablespoon of the parsley.

Add the remaining 2 tablespoons butter to the pan. Stir in the flour and cook over medium heat, stirring, for 1 minute. Gradually add 1 cup (8 fl oz/250 ml) of the hot stock, stirring constantly to prevent lumps. Add the paprika and cayenne; season to taste with salt and pepper. Simmer gently over low heat for 5 minutes.

Add 1 cup (8 fl oz/250 ml) of the remaining hot stock to the pan and simmer for 5 minutes. Gradually mix the cream into the sauce and simmer for 5–6 minutes. Stir in the remaining stock, add the chicken and simmer for 5 minutes until heated through and flavors are blended.

Transfer to a warmed platter. Garnish with the remaining 1 tablespoon parsley.

Serves 4

Chicken Breasts with Oranges

2 whole chicken breasts
3 tablespoons unsalted butter
2 oranges, peeled and sliced crosswise
½ cup (4 fl oz/125 ml) fresh orange
 juice
1 tablespoon orange zest
pinch of cayenne pepper
½ cup (4 fl oz/125 ml) heavy
 whipping (double) cream
¼ cup (2 fl oz/60 ml) dry vermouth
salt and freshly ground white pepper

Glistening sautéed orange slices top this flavorful chicken dish. Serve with sautéed mushrooms and snow peas.

Halve, skin and bone the chicken breasts as directed on pages 10–11. Trim carefully so they are all the same size; cut away any excess fat.

Melt the butter in a large sauté pan over medium heat. Add the chicken breasts and sauté, turning as they become golden, 3–4 minutes on each side.

Add the orange slices and sauté for a few minutes on each side; remove from the pan and set aside. Add the orange juice, zest and cayenne to the chicken and mix thoroughly. Cook slowly until the breasts are tender, 8–9 minutes. Remove the chicken to a warmed platter; keep warm.

Add the cream and vermouth to the pan and bring to a boil over high heat. Deglaze the pan by stirring to dislodge any browned bits. Boil for 2–3 minutes to thicken the cream. Season with salt and white pepper.

Pour the sauce over the chicken breasts and decorate each with a slice of cooked orange. Garnish the platter with the remaining orange slices.

Serves 4

Stir-Fry Chicken with Ginger

2 whole chicken breasts

2 tablespoons sesame oil

1 clove garlic

2 green (spring) onions, including tender green tops, thinly sliced lengthwise and then cut crosswise into 2-inch (5-cm) pieces

2 tablespoons chopped, peeled fresh ginger

¼ teaspoon red pepper flakes

½ cup (4 fl oz/125 ml) chicken stock (recipe on page 9)

salt and freshly ground pepper

2 tablespoons chopped crystallized ginger for garnish

The fried ginger gives a delicate Asian flavor. Serve with stir-fried spinach or snow peas, and a salad of watercress tossed with vinaigrette and small bits of orange or tangerine. Almond cookies make the perfect ending. Use a sauté pan or a wok for this super-fast dish.

*H*alve, skin and bone the chicken breasts as directed on pages 10–11. Trim off any excess fat. Place the breasts between 2 sheets of waxed paper and, using a rolling pin, flatten them slightly and evenly. Cut the halves lengthwise into strips 1 inch (2.5 cm) wide.

Warm the oil in a large sauté pan or wok over medium heat. Add the garlic and chicken and sauté the chicken, turning the pieces as they become golden, about 1 minute on each side. Stir in the green onions, fresh ginger and pepper flakes and sauté for 1–2 minutes.

Add the chicken stock and bring to a boil. Deglaze the pan by stirring to dislodge any browned bits, then reduce the heat slightly and simmer for 2–3 minutes. Season to taste with salt and pepper. Remove the garlic and discard.

Transfer the chicken and onions to a warmed platter. Pour the sauce over the top. Garnish with the crystallized ginger.

Serves 3 or 4

Oven-Braised Chicken with Vegetables

1 chicken, 3½–4 lb (1.75–2 kg)
salt
1 yellow onion, cut in half
2 leeks, including tender green tops, trimmed and carefully washed
1 head iceberg lettuce, cored and sliced lengthwise
2 carrots, peeled and coarsely chopped
2 green bell peppers (capsicums), seeded, deribbed and coarsely chopped
2 tablespoons unsalted butter, at room temperature
freshly ground pepper
½ cup (4 fl oz/125 ml) dry white wine
½ cup (4 fl oz/125 ml) chicken stock
  (recipe on page 9)

Oven braising makes chicken moist and juicy. Here you have almost an entire meal in one pot. Thin noodles or potato pancakes are good with this dish; offer fragrant melon wedges for dessert.

✻

Preheat an oven to 375°F (190°C).

Trim any excess fat from the chicken. Rub the cavity with salt and place the onion halves inside. Set aside.

Cut the leeks in half lengthwise and then thickly slice crosswise. Place the lettuce, carrots, leeks and bell peppers in the bottom of a heavy, ovenproof pot. Rub the outside of the chicken with the butter and salt and pepper to taste. Place it in the pot breast-side up. Add the wine and stock. Cover and place in the oven for 1 hour. Uncover and continue to cook until the chicken is tender, 30 minutes longer.

Transfer the chicken to a warmed deep platter. Arrange the vegetables around the bird and spoon the pan juices over it and the vegetables. Carve at the table.

Serves 4

Chicken with Garlic

1 chicken, about 3½ lb (1.75 kg)

3 tablespoons unsalted butter, at room temperature

1 teaspoon dried sage

3 whole heads garlic, separated into cloves and peeled

6 green (spring) onions, including tender green tops, sliced lengthwise

½ cup (4 fl oz/125 ml) chicken stock (*recipe on page 9*)

½ cup (4 fl oz/125 ml) dry white wine

salt and freshly ground pepper

The garlic becomes soft and mild with roasting. Spread it like butter on thinly sliced warm bread and eat with the chicken. Serve with mashed potatoes and coleslaw or sautéed zucchini (courgettes) with their blossoms.

Preheat an oven to 375°F (190°C).

Trim any excess fat from the chicken. Rub the cavity with 1 tablespoon of the butter and then sprinkle the cavity with the sage. Place 8 of the garlic cloves inside.

Rub 1 tablespoon of the butter on the bottom of a roasting pan. Scatter the green onions over the bottom and place the chicken on the bed of onions. Rub the entire surface of the chicken with the remaining 1 tablespoon butter. Place the bird on its side and tuck garlic cloves around the chicken and under the wings.

Place in the oven and roast for 30 minutes. Turn the bird so it rests on its opposite side. Combine the stock and wine and stir ½ cup (4 fl oz/125 ml) of it into the pan. Baste the chicken and roast for another 30 minutes.

Add the remaining ½ cup (4 fl oz/125 ml) stock-wine mixture. Turn the chicken breast-side up, baste with the pan juices, and season to taste with salt and pepper. Roast until the chicken is tender and golden, another 20–30 minutes.

Transfer the chicken to a warmed platter with the garlic cloves. Carve at the table.

Serves 4

Chicken Casserole with Green Noodles

2 chickens, about 2 lb (1 kg) each,
  quartered (see page 10)
¼ cup (2 oz/60 g) unsalted butter
1 tablespoon dried sage
salt and freshly ground pepper
1 lb (500 g) dried green noodles
2 cups (16 fl oz/500 ml) heavy
  whipping (double) cream
¼ cup (2 fl oz/60 ml) dry sherry
¼ cup (1 oz/30 g) freshly grated
  Parmesan cheese
¼ cup (1 oz/30 g) freshly grated
  Fontina cheese

Casseroles are ideal for the cook who likes to entertain, because they usually demand a minimum of last-minute attention and can be assembled in advance. All that is needed is a salad and dessert. Don't forget warm bread and wine.

*P*reheat an oven to 350°F (180°C).

Trim any excess fat from the chicken. Place in a 1½-qt (48 fl oz/1.5 l) ovenproof casserole or baking dish. Butter the chicken pieces on all sides and then sprinkle with the sage. Arrange skin-side down.

Place in the oven and bake for 15 minutes. Turn the chicken pieces over, season to taste with salt and pepper, cover and bake for another 15 minutes. Meanwhile, bring a large pot of water to a boil. Add the noodles and cook until barely tender. Drain and set aside.

Remove the chicken from the casserole and set aside. Pour off the excess oil from the casserole. In a saucepan gently warm the cream and sherry; add to the casserole and stir to blend. Add the noodles to the cream mixture and sprinkle with half of each of the cheeses. Arrange the chicken on top of the noodles and sprinkle the remaining cheese over the top. Cover and bake until the chicken is tender and the sauce is bubbling, about 20 minutes. Serve directly from the casserole.

Serves 4–6

Lemon Chicken

1 chicken, about 3½ lb (1.75 kg)
2 teaspoons dried tarragon
3 lemons
¼ cup (2 oz/60 g) unsalted butter
2 tablespoons Dijon mustard
4 yellow onions, cut in half crosswise
2 tablespoons balsamic vinegar
½ cup (4 fl oz/125 ml) chicken stock
  (*recipe on page 9*)
salt and freshly ground pepper
1 bunch watercress

The golden chicken, infused with the aroma of lemon, is served on a bed of watercress to catch the delicious juices. Roasted onions glazed with balsamic vinegar add a strong accent.

Preheat an oven to 375°F (190°C).

Trim any excess fat from the chicken. Sprinkle the cavity with 1 teaspoon of the tarragon. Cut 1 lemon in half and place a lemon half in the cavity.

Squeeze the remaining lemons; you should have about ¼ cup (2 fl oz/60 ml) juice. Melt the butter in a small pan over medium heat. Stir in the lemon juice, the remaining 1 teaspoon tarragon and the mustard; mix well. Brush some of the butter mixture over the surface of the chicken. Place breast-side down in a shallow roasting pan. Arrange the onions around the chicken; brush half of the remaining butter mixture over the onions. Roast in the oven for 30 minutes.

Spoon the vinegar over the onions and stir the stock into the pan. Baste the chicken with the pan juices and roast for another 30 minutes. Turn the chicken breast-side up, baste with the remaining butter mixture and season with salt and pepper. Continue to roast until the chicken is tender and golden, another 20–30 minutes.

Make a bed of watercress on a warmed platter. Place the bird on top and surround with the onions. Baste the chicken with some of the pan juices; serve the remaining juices on the side. Carve the chicken at the table.

Serves 4

Chicken with Wine and Grapes

1 chicken, about 3½ lb (1.75 kg),
   quartered (see page 10)
1 lemon, cut in half
2 teaspoons dried sage
3 tablespoons olive oil
4 shallots, cut in half lengthwise
½ cup (4 fl oz/125 ml) chicken stock
   (recipe on page 9)
½ cup (4 fl oz/125 ml) dry white wine
3 small bunches grapes (mixture of
   green and red)
salt and freshly ground pepper
2 tablespoons brandy

In late summer, grapes mature and hang from the vines in plump bunches—green, amber, deep red and black. The Italians in the Chianti region of northern Italy bake chicken with grapes and wine. Look for fresh sage to add as a garnish.

*P*reheat an oven to 375°F (190°C).

Trim any excess fat from the chicken. Rub with the cut side of a lemon half and sprinkle the sage on both sides of the chicken pieces.

Place in a shallow baking dish, skin-side down, and drizzle with the oil. Place 2 shallot halves in the hollow of each chicken quarter.

Place in the oven and bake for 20 minutes. In a small saucepan, gently heat the stock and wine. Stir ½ cup (4 fl oz/125 ml) of the mixture into the bottom of the dish. Baste the chicken with the pan juices. Turn skin-side up and arrange the grapes around the chicken. Bake for 30 minutes longer, basting a few times with the remaining stock mixture. Season with salt and pepper.

Pour the brandy into a small saucepan and warm gently. Using a long-handled match, ignite the brandy. When the flame dies, pour the brandy evenly over the chicken and grapes. Baste the chicken and grapes with the pan juices. Bake until golden brown, 15–20 minutes.

Transfer the chicken to a warmed platter with the grapes arranged around the sides. Strain the sauce and serve in a bowl on the side.

Serves 4

Chicken with Bell Peppers and Parmesan

1 chicken, 3–4 lb (1.5–2 kg),
  quartered (see page 10)
3 tablespoons olive oil
1 teaspoon dried sage
1 teaspoon dried thyme
3 tomatoes, chopped
2 red bell peppers (capsicums),
  seeded, deribbed and cut into long,
  wide strips
½ cup (4 fl oz/125 ml) chicken stock,
  heated (recipe on page 9)
½ cup (4 fl oz/125 ml) dry red wine
½ cup (2 oz/60 g) freshly grated
  Parmesan or Romano cheese
freshly ground pepper

The perfect chicken dish: simple to prepare and delicious to eat. A yellow bell pepper makes a colorful addition. Serve with crusty bread and braised fennel, or white beans mixed with oil and finely chopped green (spring) onions and parsley.

Preheat an oven to 375°F (190°C).

Trim any excess fat from the chicken. Place in a baking dish or pan; brush the bottom and the chicken with 2 tablespoons of the oil. Turn the chicken quarters skin-side down and sprinkle with the sage and thyme.

Place in the oven and bake for 20 minutes. Baste the chicken with the pan juices. Add the tomatoes, bell peppers, hot chicken stock and wine and bake for another 20 minutes, basting occasionally. Turn the chicken skin-side up, sprinkle the cheese over the top and season to taste with pepper. Place in the upper one-third of the oven and bake until the chicken is browned and tender, another 20 minutes.

Transfer the chicken to a warmed platter and spoon the pan juices and vegetables around it.

Serves 4

Rosemary Chicken with Potatoes

1 chicken, about 3½ lb (1.75 kg)

1 lemon, cut in half

6 fresh rosemary sprigs

4 russet potatoes, peeled and cut into 2-inch (5-cm) cubes

3 tablespoons unsalted butter

3 tablespoons olive oil

2 teaspoons dried rosemary

1 teaspoon dried thyme

½ cup (4 fl oz/125 ml) chicken stock (recipe on page 9)

salt and freshly ground pepper

The chicken and potatoes absorb the rosemary's fragrance. Truss the chicken (see page 15) and tuck sprigs of fresh rosemary under the wings. Serve with a green salad tossed with chopped celery, radishes and chives. For a large dinner party, roast two birds.

Preheat an oven to 350°F (180°C).

Trim any excess fat from the chicken. Rub inside and out with a lemon half. Place 2 rosemary sprigs in the cavity and tuck 1 rosemary sprig under each wing. Place the chicken on its side in a roasting pan and surround with the potatoes. Melt the butter in a small pan and stir in the oil. Brush the butter mixture evenly over the chicken and potatoes and then sprinkle with the dried rosemary and thyme.

Place in the oven and roast for 30 minutes. Turn the chicken so it rests on its opposite side. Add the stock to the pan and baste the chicken with the pan juices. Roast for another 30 minutes. Turn the chicken breast-side up, baste with the pan juices and season to taste with salt and pepper. Roast until the chicken is tender, another 20–30 minutes.

Transfer the chicken to a warmed platter and surround with the potatoes. Garnish with the 2 remaining rosemary sprigs. Serve the pan juices in a bowl on the side. Carve the chicken at the table.

Serves 4

Chicken and Eggplant Casserole

2 chickens, about 2½ lb (1.25 kg)
   each, quartered (see page 10)
3 tablespoons brandy
4 tablespoons (2 fl oz/60 ml) olive oil
2 cloves garlic, cut in half
salt and freshly ground pepper
2 cups (1 lb/500 g) chopped red and
   yellow bell peppers (capsicums)
4 tomatoes, cut into quarters
1 small eggplant (aubergine), cut
   lengthwise into sticks ¼ inch
   (6 mm) thick
1 cup (8 fl oz/250 ml) chicken stock,
   heated (recipe on page 9)
1 teaspoon dried thyme
2 bay leaves
½ cup (4 fl oz/125 ml) dry white wine
1 tablespoon chopped fresh parsley or
   cilantro (fresh coriander)

Make this casserole when peppers and tomatoes are at their best. Serve with hot garlic bread and a salad of shredded celery root (celeriac).

Preheat an oven to 375°F (190°C).

Trim any excess fat from the chicken. Place the chicken quarters in a 1½-qt (48 fl oz/1.5 l) ovenproof casserole or baking dish and brush them with the brandy. Add 2 tablespoons of the oil and the garlic to the casserole and place the chicken skin-side down. Place in the oven for 10 minutes to brown. Turn skin-side up and bake for 10 minutes longer. Season to taste with salt and pepper.

Meanwhile, in a frying pan warm the remaining 2 tablespoons oil over medium heat. Add the peppers and sauté for 2 minutes. Add the tomatoes and eggplant and cook for 5 minutes, stirring occasionally. Pour off the oil. Pour in ½ cup (4 fl oz/125 ml) of the hot stock and add the thyme and bay leaves. Simmer until the vegetables soften slightly, 3–4 minutes. Remove from the heat.

Spoon the vegetable mixture around the chicken in the casserole. Add the remaining ½ cup (4 fl oz/125 ml) hot stock and the white wine. Cover and bake until the chicken is tender, about 40 minutes.

Sprinkle the parsley or cilantro over the top and serve directly from the casserole.

Serves 4–6

Chicken with Plum Jam and Almonds

1 chicken, about 3½ lb (1.75 kg)
2 tablespoons sesame oil
½ cup (5 oz/150 g) plum jam
2 tablespoons grated fresh ginger
1 tablespoon fresh lemon juice
2 tablespoons dry sherry
2 tablespoons red wine vinegar
½ cup (4 fl oz/125 ml) chicken stock,
   heated (recipe on page 9)
½ cup (2 oz/60 g) chopped almonds
fresh cilantro (fresh coriander) for
   garnish

A lovely Chinese-inspired combination of plums and chicken in a sweet-and-sour sauce with ginger and almonds. Serve with Chinese-style green beans and celery cut on the diagonal and cooked briefly in stock.

Preheat an oven to 325°F (165°C).

Cut the chicken into 8 pieces as directed on pages 10–11. Trim off any excess fat.

Warm the oil in a large sauté pan over medium heat. Add the chicken and sauté, turning the pieces as they become golden, 3–4 minutes on each side. Remove to a baking dish and set aside.

In a small bowl combine the jam, ginger, lemon juice, sherry and vinegar and stir to mix well. Spoon some of the jam mixture over each chicken piece and turn to coat on both sides.

Place in the oven and bake for 25–30 minutes. Add the hot stock to the pan juices and continue to bake, basting frequently with the pan juices, until the chicken is tender, another 20–25 minutes.

Place the chicken on a warmed platter. Dust with the chopped almonds and garnish with the cilantro.

Serves 2 or 3

Chicken and Brown Rice Pilaf

3½ cups (28 fl oz/875 ml) chicken stock (recipe on page 9)

1½ cups (8 oz/250 g) long-grain brown rice

½ cup (3 oz/90 g) raisins

1 cup (8 fl oz/250 ml) fresh orange juice

3 tablespoons olive oil or sesame oil

½ teaspoon ground ginger

½ cup (3 oz/90 g) chopped green (spring) onions

8 chicken legs

¼ cup (1 oz/30 g) grated orange zest

½ cup (3 oz/90 g) pine nuts

2 tablespoons finely chopped fresh mint

This pilaf has a Middle Eastern influence and is made with an interesting mix of ingredients: pine nuts, orange juice and zest, raisins, ginger and fresh mint. Assemble it in advance and slip it into the oven whenever you wish.

*P*reheat an oven to 350°F (180°C).

In a 1½-qt (48 fl oz/1.5 l) ovenproof casserole or baking dish, combine 3 cups (24 fl oz/750 ml) of the chicken stock and the brown rice. Cover and place in the oven for 40 minutes.

Meanwhile, in a small bowl combine the raisins and orange juice and set aside to soak.

Warm the oil in a sauté pan over medium heat. Stir in the ginger and onions and sauté for 1 minute. Add the chicken legs and sauté, turning as they become golden, 3–4 minutes on each side. Remove the chicken; set aside.

Pour off the oil from the pan. Add the remaining ½ cup (4 fl oz/125 ml) stock and bring to a boil. Deglaze the pan by stirring to dislodge any browned bits.

Remove the casserole from the oven and stir the onion-stock mixture into the rice. Mix in the raisins, orange juice, orange zest and pine nuts. Add the chicken, cover and return to the oven. Bake for 30 minutes.

Sprinkle with the mint and serve directly from the casserole.

Serves 4–6

Savory Chicken with Sausages

2 chickens, about 2½ lb (1.25 kg) each, cut in half lengthwise (see page 10)
3 tablespoons olive oil
2 cloves garlic, cut in half
1 teaspoon dried thyme
1 teaspoon dried sage
2 tablespoons fresh lemon juice
6 mild Italian sausages, 1½ lb (750 g) total weight
1 cup (8 fl oz/250 ml) dry white wine
salt and freshly ground pepper
6 fresh parsley sprigs for garnish

The sausages season the chicken with a wonderful spicy tang. Serve with sautéed fresh vegetables, baked apples and a salad of green leaf lettuce and chicory (curly endive).

Preheat an oven to 375°F (190°C). Trim any excess fat from the chicken.

In a small bowl combine the oil, garlic, thyme, sage and lemon juice and stir to mix well. Brush over both sides of each chicken half and brush any remaining herb mixture on the bottom of a roasting pan. Place the chicken halves in the pan skin-side down. Arrange the sausages around the chicken.

Place in the oven and roast for 20 minutes. Turn the chicken halves skin-side up, stir the wine into the pan juices and baste the chicken. Continue to roast, basting frequently, until the chicken is tender and golden, another 20–30 minutes. Season with salt and pepper.

Carve the chicken and transfer to a warmed platter. Slice the sausages and arrange them around the chicken. Garnish with the parsley sprigs.

Serves 4

Chicken Breasts Stuffed with Herbs, Green Peppercorns and Prosciutto

2 whole chicken breasts

4 slices prosciutto

1 tablespoon green peppercorns, crushed

1 clove garlic, chopped

¼ cup (2 fl oz/60 ml) olive oil

3 tablespoons chopped fresh parsley

2 tablespoons chopped fresh basil or 1 tablespoon dried basil

salt and freshly ground pepper

16 fresh mushrooms

½ cup (4 fl oz/125 ml) chicken stock, heated *(recipe on page 9)*

These are also good the next day sliced thin and served cold with green parsley sauce (recipe on page 13).

Preheat an oven to 350°F (180°C).

Halve, skin and bone the chicken breasts as directed on pages 10–11. Trim off any excess fat. Place between 2 sheets of waxed paper and, using a rolling pin, flatten until the meat is of an even thickness, about ¼ inch (6 mm). Place 1 prosciutto slice on each breast half.

In a bowl combine the crushed green peppercorns, garlic, oil, 2 tablespoons of the parsley, the basil and salt and pepper to taste. Stir to mix thoroughly. Place 1 tablespoon of the parsley mixture on each prosciutto slice; roll up each breast and secure with 2 toothpicks. Arrange the rolled breasts, seam-side down, in a baking dish. Surround the rolls with the mushrooms and spoon the remaining herb mixture over the chicken and mushrooms.

Place in the oven and bake for 15 minutes. Pour the hot stock into the dish and baste the chicken and mushrooms. Continue baking, basting frequently with the pan juices, until the chicken is tender, another 20–25 minutes.

Place the chicken breasts and mushrooms on a warmed platter and spoon the pan juices over top. Sprinkle with the remaining 1 tablespoon parsley.

Serves 4

Greek Chicken with Oregano

2 chickens, about 2½ lb (1.25 kg) each, cut in half lengthwise (see page 10)
½ cup (4 fl oz/125 ml) olive oil
juice of 2 lemons
2 tablespoons dried oregano
2 yellow onions, chopped
4 cloves garlic, chopped
salt and freshly ground pepper
about 1 cup (8 fl oz/250 ml) dry white wine
1 bunch spinach, trimmed and washed
4 fresh oregano sprigs

The Greeks use a great deal of oregano in their cooking, particularly in chicken dishes. A mixed vegetable salad and oven-broiled potato slices are delicious accompaniments to these succulent birds.

*P*reheat an oven to 400°F (200°C).

Trim any excess fat from the chicken. In a small bowl combine the oil, lemon juice and dried oregano and stir to mix well. Brush the mixture over both sides of each chicken half, including under the wings. Place in a roasting pan, skin-side down. Tuck the onions and garlic in the hollows of the chicken pieces and season to taste with salt and pepper.

Place in the oven and roast for 20 minutes. Turn the chicken halves skin-side up, stir ½ cup (4 fl oz/125 ml) of the wine into the pan juices and baste the chicken. Continue to roast, basting frequently with the pan juices, until tender and golden, another 30 minutes. Add more wine to the pan as needed to keep the chicken moist.

Arrange a bed of spinach leaves on a warmed platter and place the chicken on top. Strain the pan juices and pour over the chicken. Garnish with the oregano sprigs.

Serves 4

French Chicken with Prunes

2 chickens, about 2½ lb (1.25 kg)
  each, quartered (see page 10)
2 tablespoons unsalted butter, at room
  temperature
1 teaspoon dried thyme
½ cup (4 fl oz/125 ml) fresh orange
  juice
½ cup (4 fl oz/125 ml) dry white wine
12 prunes, pitted
½ cup (4 fl oz/125 ml) chicken stock,
  heated (recipe on page 9)
3 carrots, peeled and cut into slices
  ¼ inch (6 mm) thick
2 tablespoons brandy
salt and freshly ground pepper

A pretty wintertime supper dish with the contrasting colors of carrots and prunes. Good with braised fennel or an orange, onion and avocado salad, and winter pears for dessert.

*P*reheat an oven to 375°F (190°C).

Trim any excess fat from the chicken. Butter the chicken pieces on both sides and then sprinkle with the thyme. Arrange in a baking dish, skin-side down. Place in the oven and bake for 20 minutes.

Meanwhile, in a saucepan combine the orange juice and wine and bring to a boil over high heat. Reduce the heat, add the prunes, cover and simmer until soft, 8–10 minutes.

When the chicken has baked for 20 minutes, turn the pieces skin-side up, stir the hot stock into the pan juices and baste the chicken. Using a slotted spoon, transfer the cooked prunes to the baking dish. Add ½ cup (4 fl oz/ 125 ml) of their cooking liquid to the dish juices. Scatter the carrots around the chicken. Bake until the chicken is tender, 40–50 minutes. During the last 10 minutes of cooking, add the brandy to the juices and season to taste with salt and pepper.

Place the chicken, prunes and carrots on a warmed platter. Spoon the pan juices over all.

Serves 4

Chicken Legs with Chutney

8 chicken legs

1 lemon, cut in half

5 tablespoons (2½ oz/80 g) unsalted
butter, at room temperature

2 teaspoons curry powder

2 tablespoons Dijon mustard

3½ tablespoons mango chutney

freshly ground pepper

½ cup (4 fl oz/125 ml) dry white
wine, heated

4 fresh thyme sprigs for garnish,
optional

*Brown rice cooked with thyme, raisins and sliced bananas
complements these well-seasoned drumsticks nicely. Chilled
mango with lime juice provides the perfect finish.*

*P*reheat an oven to 350°F (180°C).

Skin the chicken legs and trim off any excess fat. Using
a sharp knife, score the chicken legs so the chutney
mixture will be absorbed into the cuts. Place the legs in a
baking dish and squeeze the juice of ½ lemon over them.

In a small bowl mix together the butter, curry powder,
mustard and the juice from the remaining lemon half.
Stir in the chutney and season to taste with pepper. Coat
the chicken with the mixture to cover completely.

Place in the oven and roast for 15 minutes. Pour the
warm wine into the dish and baste the chicken with the
pan juices. Continue to roast, turning the legs to brown
them on both sides and basting occasionally with the
pan juices, until tender, about 30 minutes.

Transfer the chicken to a warmed platter and garnish
with the thyme, if desired. Serve at once.

Serves 4

Chicken and Broccoli Casserole

3 whole chicken breasts

½ cup (2 oz/60 g) all-purpose (plain) flour

1 tablespoon dried sage

1 teaspoon paprika

3 tablespoons unsalted butter

2 cups (6 oz/180 g) chopped broccoli

6 thin slices lean boiled ham

1 cup (8 fl oz/250 ml) heavy whipping (double) cream

¼ cup (2 fl oz/60 ml) sherry

½ cup (2 oz/60 g) freshly grated Parmesan or Romano cheese

salt and freshly ground pepper

This dish comes to the table with the sauce golden and bubbling. Make an enormous green salad and a rich chocolate dessert and your guests are certain to be content.

Preheat an oven to 350°F (180°C).

Halve, skin and bone the chicken breasts as directed on pages 10–11. Trim off any excess fat.

Mix the flour, sage and paprika together in a sturdy paper bag. Drop each chicken piece into the bag and shake to coat on all sides. Shake off any excess.

Melt the butter in a sauté pan over medium heat. Add the chicken pieces and sauté, turning as they become golden, 3–4 minutes on each side. Remove the chicken and set aside. Leave the pan on the stove.

Arrange the broccoli in a layer in the bottom of a baking dish. Cover with the browned chicken and top each chicken piece with a slice of ham.

Pour off the excess oil from the sauté pan and add the cream. Bring to a boil over high heat. Deglaze the pan by stirring to dislodge any browned bits. Add the sherry and boil for 2 minutes. Stir in all but 2 tablespoons of the cheese and season to taste with salt and pepper. Remove from the heat. Top each piece of ham with a large spoonful of the cream sauce and pour the remaining sauce around the chicken. Sprinkle the reserved 2 tablespoons cheese over the top.

Place in the oven and bake until the chicken is tender and the sauce is bubbling, 30–40 minutes. Serve directly from the baking dish.

Serves 4–6

Broiled Chicken with Vinaigrette

2 chickens, about 2½ lb (1.25 kg) each, cut in half lengthwise (see page 10)
¼ cup (2 fl oz/60 ml) sesame oil
¼ cup (2 fl oz/60 ml) olive oil
1 tablespoon Dijon mustard
¼ cup (2 fl oz/60 ml) dry vermouth
1 cup (4 oz/120 g) dried bread crumbs
salt and freshly ground pepper
1 head butter lettuce, separated into leaves

FOR THE MINT VINAIGRETTE:
½ cup (4 fl oz/125 ml) sesame oil
¼ cup (2 fl oz/60 ml) red wine vinegar
2 tablespoons finely chopped fresh mint
1 tablespoon soy sauce
½ teaspoon ground coriander

This golden chicken is served on a bed of lettuce with mint vinaigrette—a cool contrast to the crisp chicken.

❧

*P*reheat a broiler (griller). Trim any excess fat from the chicken.

In a small bowl stir together the sesame and olive oils, mustard and vermouth. Brush the chicken halves with some of the mixture and place skin-side down in a shallow flameproof baking dish. Slip under the hot broiler about 4 inches (10 cm) from the heat and broil (grill) for 15 minutes. Turn the chicken over, baste with the dish juices and broil for another 15 minutes.

Spread the bread crumbs on a sheet of waxed paper and season to taste with salt and pepper. Remove the chicken from the broiler, brush the skin side with the remaining oil-mustard mixture and roll the skin side in the bread crumbs. Return the chicken to the dish skin-side up and return to the broiler. Broil until dark golden brown, 4–5 minutes.

Meanwhile, arrange the lettuce leaves on a platter; use only the small inner leaves and save the others for another use. In a small bowl stir together all the vinaigrette ingredients. Drizzle about ¼ cup (2 fl oz/ 60 ml) over the lettuce. Place the chicken pieces on the lettuce and spoon about 2 tablespoons of the vinaigrette over each piece.

Serves 4–6

Chicken Kebabs

2 whole chicken breasts
1 cup (8 fl oz/250 ml) olive oil
4 cloves garlic, cut in half
2 tablespoons soy sauce
½ cup (1 oz/30 g) chopped fresh basil
1 lemon, cut in half
8 large fresh mushrooms, thickly
   sliced
1 red (Spanish) onion, thickly sliced
salt and freshly ground pepper
4 fresh basil or mint sprigs for garnish

The long, balmy evenings of summer inspire outdoor grilling and entertaining, and these kebabs can make the move to a charcoal fire. Feel free to use your favorite summer vegetables, such as yellow summer squash and bell peppers (capsicums). If you use wooden skewers, soak them well and keep them from direct contact with the flame. Offer tomato-cranberry salsa and red pepper sauce (recipes on page 13) on the side. Serve the skewers atop a bed of rice pilaf, if you like.

Preheat a broiler (griller). Skin and bone the chicken breasts as directed on pages 10–11. Trim off any excess fat. Cut the meat into 2-inch (5-cm) squares; you should have 32 in all.

In a large bowl stir together the oil, garlic, soy sauce, chopped basil and the juice of ½ lemon. Add the chicken and vegetables and toss to coat lightly.

Load eight 12-inch (30-cm) skewers with the chicken pieces, mushrooms and onion. Reserve the oil mixture.

Arrange the skewers in a shallow flameproof baking dish. Slip under the hot broiler about 4 inches (10 cm) from the heat. Broil (grill), turning the skewers to brown all sides and basting occasionally with the reserved oil mixture, until the vegetables and chicken are tender, 10–12 minutes. Season to taste with salt and pepper.

Squeeze the juice from the remaining lemon half over the chicken and vegetables; garnish with the herb sprigs.

Serves 4

Broiled Chicken with Herb-Stuffed Breast

2 young chickens, about 2 lb (1 kg) each, cut in half lengthwise (see page 10)

½ cup (4 oz/125 g) unsalted butter, at room temperature

½ cup (¾ oz/20 g) chopped fresh parsley

4 tablespoons chopped fresh chives

1 teaspoon dried tarragon

salt and freshly ground pepper

4 slices toast, buttered

4 tablespoons (3 oz/90 g) apricot or peach chutney

This is a springtime dish. The herb-infused chickens can be served with your choice of young, tender vegetables. Offer two sauces on the side: horseradish-mustard sauce and green parsley sauce (recipes on page 13).

Preheat a broiler (griller). Trim any excess fat from the chicken.

In a small bowl combine the butter, parsley, chives, tarragon and salt and pepper to taste. Stir until well mixed. Following the directions on page 15, loosen the skin covering the breast on each chicken half. Spread 1 tablespoon of the butter-herb mixture evenly between the skin and breast of each chicken half.

Melt the remaining butter-herb mixture. Brush some of it on both sides of the chicken halves and place skin-side down in a shallow flameproof baking dish. Slip under the hot broiler about 3 inches (7.5 cm) from the heat and broil (grill) for 15 minutes.

Turn the chicken skin-side up, brush with the remaining melted butter mixture and the pan juices, and broil until tender and golden brown, about 12 minutes. Season to taste with salt and pepper.

Place the buttered toasts on a platter and spoon 1 tablespoon chutney on each slice. Arrange a chicken half atop each toast. Serve at once.

Serves 4

Chicken on Skewers Provençal

2 cloves garlic, cut in half
½ cup (4 fl oz/125 ml) olive oil
salt and freshly ground pepper
1 teaspoon dried rosemary
1 teaspoon dried thyme
8 chicken thighs
1 eggplant (aubergine), cut into
  sixteen 2-inch (5-cm) cubes
8 fresh rosemary sprigs, dipped into
  olive oil
8 plum (Roma) tomatoes, cut in half

These skewers can also be done on the outdoor grill. If you use wooden skewers, soak them in water before using.

In a large, shallow bowl combine the garlic, oil, salt and pepper to taste, rosemary and thyme.

Skin and bone the chicken thighs as directed on pages 10–11; trim off any excess fat. Slit the underside of each thigh, if necessary, so the meat lies flat. Add the meat to the oil mixture and coat well. Let stand at room temperature for 1 hour, turning frequently.

Preheat a broiler (griller). Remove the chicken from the marinade; reserve the marinade. Cut each thigh in half; you should have sixteen 2-inch (5-cm) squares in all. Load each of eight 12-inch (30-cm) skewers in the following manner: 1 eggplant cube, 1 chicken square, 1 rosemary sprig, 1 tomato half, 1 eggplant cube, 1 chicken square, 1 tomato half.

Arrange the skewers in a shallow flameproof baking dish. Slip under the hot broiler about 4 inches (10 cm) from the heat. Broil (grill), turning the skewers to brown all sides and basting occasionally with the reserved marinade, until the chicken and vegetables are tender, 10–12 minutes. Season to taste with salt and pepper.

Slip the vegetables and chicken from the skewers onto a warmed platter. Garnish with the grilled rosemary sprigs.

Serves 4

Glossary

The following glossary defines terms specifically as they relate to chicken cookery, including major and unusual ingredients and basic techniques.

ARUGULA
Green leaf vegetable, Mediterranean in origin, with slender, multiple-lobed leaves that have a peppery, slightly bitter flavor. Often used raw in salads; also known as rocket.

BASIL
Sweet, spicy herb popular in Italian and French cooking, particularly as a seasoning for **tomatoes** and tomato sauces.

BASTE
To spoon or otherwise pour pan juices over food while it roasts, promoting moistness and a richly colored, well-browned surface. Basting should be performed at regular intervals when roasting chicken.

BAY LEAVES
Dried whole leaves of the bay laurel tree. Pungent and spicy, they flavor simmered dishes, marinades and pickling mixtures. The French variety, sometimes available in specialty-food shops, has a milder, sweeter flavor than California bay leaves. Before serving any dish in which bay leaves were used as a seasoning, discard the leaves.

BELGIAN ENDIVE
Leaf vegetable with refreshing, slightly bitter spear-shaped leaves, white to pale yellow green—or sometimes red—in color, tightly packed in cylindrical heads 4–6 inches (10–15 cm) long. Also known as chicory or witloof.

BELL PEPPER
Fresh, sweet-fleshed, bell-shaped member of the pepper family; also known as capsicum. Most common in the unripe green form, although ripened red or yellow varieties are also available. Creamy pale-yellow, orange and purple-black types may also be found.

To prepare a raw bell pepper, begin by cutting it in half lengthwise with a sharp knife. Using your fingers, pull out the stem section from each half, along with the cluster of seeds attached to it. Remove any remaining seeds, along with any thin white ribs to which they are attached. Cut the pepper halves into quarters, strips or thin slices, as called for in the recipe.

BRANDY
Applies to any spirit distilled from fermented fruit juice, but most specifically to dry grape brandy—the finest of which is generally acknowledged to be Cognac, from the French region of the same name.

BUTTER LETTUCE
Relatively small type of round lettuce with soft, loosely packed, tender, mildly flavored leaves. Also known as Boston lettuce. Butter lettuce is a member of the butterhead family, which also includes the Bibb, or limestone, variety.

CALVADOS
Dry French brandy distilled from apples and bearing the fruit's distinctive aroma and taste. Dry applejack may be substituted.

CAPERS
Small, pickled buds of a bush common to the Mediterranean, used whole as a savory flavoring or garnish. The salty, sharp-tasting brine may also be used as a seasoning.

CAYENNE PEPPER
Very hot ground spice derived from dried cayenne chili pepper.

CELERY HEART
The small, partially formed inner stalks of a head of celery, prized for their tenderness and mild, sweet flavor.

CHIVES
Long, thin green herb with a mild, sweet flavor reminiscent of the **onion,** to which it is related. Although chives are available dried in the spice section of a supermarket, fresh chives possess the best flavor.

CHUTNEY
Refers to any number of spiced East Indian–style relishes or pickles served as condiments with meals and used as seasonings in cooking; most common are fruit-based chutneys, particularly mango. Available in ethnic markets, specialty-food stores and supermarket Asian-food sections.

CILANTRO
Green, leafy herb resembling flat-leaf (Italian) **parsley,** with a sharp, aromatic, somewhat astringent flavor. Popular in Latin American and Asian cuisines. Also called fresh coriander and commonly referred to as Chinese parsley.

COCONUT MILK
Though commonly thought to be the thin, relatively clear liquid found inside a whole coconut, coconut milk in cooking is actually an extract made from shredded fresh coconut. Sold in cans in ethnic markets.

CRANBERRIES
Round, deep red, tartly acidic berries, grown primarily in wet, sandy coastal lands—or bogs—in the northeastern United States. Available fresh during the late autumn, and frozen year-round.

CURRY POWDER
Generic term for blends of spices commonly used to flavor Indian-style dishes. Most curry powders include coriander, cumin, chili powder, fenugreek and turmeric; other additions may include cardamom, cinnamon, cloves, allspice, **fennel** seeds and **ginger.** Best purchased in small quantities, because flavor diminishes rapidly after opening.

DEGLAZE
To dissolve the thin glaze of juices and browned bits on the surface of a pan in which food has been fried, sautéed or roasted. To do this, add liquid and stir and scrape over high heat, thereby adding flavor to the liquid for use as a sauce.

EGGPLANT

Vegetable-fruit, also known as aubergine, with tender, mildly earthy, sweet flesh. The shiny skins of eggplants vary in color from purple to red and from yellow to white, and their shapes range from small and oval to long

and slender to large and pear shaped. The most common variety is large, purple and globular; but slender, purple Asian eggplants, more tender and with fewer, smaller seeds, are available with increasing frequency in supermarkets and vegetable markets.

FENNEL

Crisp, refreshing, mildly anise-flavored bulb vegetable, sometimes called by its Italian name, *finocchio*. Also valued for its fine, feathery leaves, which are used as a fresh or dried herb, and for its small, crescent-shaped seeds, dried and used whole as a spice.

FONTINA

Creamy, mild-tasting Italian cheese made from sheep's milk.

GINGER

The rhizome of the tropical ginger plant, which yields a sweet, strong-flavored spice. The whole rhizome may be purchased fresh in a supermarket or vegetable market. Pieces of it may be found crystallized or candied in specialty-food shops or supermarket baking sections, or preserved in syrup in specialty-food shops or Asian-food sections. Dried and ground ginger is commonly available in jars or tins in the spice section.

HORSERADISH

Pungent, hot-tasting root, a member of the mustard family, sold fresh and whole, or already grated and bottled as a prepared sauce. The best prepared horseradish is the freshly grated variety, bottled in a light vinegar and found in the refrigerated section of the supermarket.

JALAPEÑO PEPPER

Extremely hot fresh chili pepper with a distinctively sharp flavor. It has a broad, tapering body that measures about 1½ inches (4 cm) long and is usually dark green, although ripe red jalapeños are occasionally available.

MARJORAM

Pungent, aromatic herb used dried or fresh to season meats (particularly lamb), poultry, seafood, vegetables and eggs.

MINT

Refreshing sweet herb used fresh to flavor lamb, poultry, vegetables and fruits.

MUSTARD, DIJON

Mustard made in Dijon, France, from dark brown mustard seeds (unless otherwise marked "blanc") and white wine or wine vinegar. Pale in color, fairly hot and sharp-tasting, true Dijon mustard and non-French blends labeled "Dijon style" are available in supermarkets and specialty-food stores.

LEEK

Sweet, moderately flavored member of the onion family, long and cylindrical in shape with a pale white root end and dark green leaves. Select firm, unblemished leeks, small to medium in size. Grown in sandy soil, the leafy-topped, multi-layered vegetables require thorough cleaning.

Trim off the tough ends of the dark green leaves. Trim off the roots. If a recipe calls for leek whites only, trim off the dark green leaves where they meet the slender pale-green part of the stem. Starting about 1 inch (2.5 cm) from the root end, slit the leek lengthwise.

Vigorously swish the leek in a basin or sink filled with cold water. Drain and rinse again; check to make sure that no dirt remains between the tightly packed pale portion of the leaves.

To slice a leek, hold it steadily on a cutting surface and, using a sharp knife, cut crosswise starting at the root end. If a recipe calls for chopped leek, simply chop the slices.

OIL, OLIVE

Extra-virgin olive oil, extracted from olives on the first pressing without use of heat or chemicals, is preferred. Many brands, varying in color and strength of flavor, are now available; select one that suits your taste. The higher-priced extra-virgin olive oils are usually of better quality. Store in an airtight container away from heat and light.

OIL, SESAME

Rich, flavorful and aromatic oil pressed from sesame seeds. Those from China and Japan are usually made with toasted sesame seeds, resulting in a darker, stronger oil used as a flavoring ingredient; its low burning temperature makes it unsuitable for using alone for cooking. Middle Eastern and Western forms of the oil, made from untoasted seeds, are lighter in color and taste, and may be used for cooking.

OLIVES, BLACK

Throughout Mediterranean Europe, ripe black olives are cured in various combinations of salt, seasonings, brines, vinegars and oils to produce a range of pungently flavored results. Good-quality cured olives are available in ethnic delicatessens, specialty-food shops and well-stocked supermarkets.

OLIVES, GREEN
Olives picked in their unripened, green state and cured in brine—sometimes with seasonings, vinegars and oils—to produce results generally more sharp tasting than ripe black olives. Sold in ethnic delicatessens, specialty-food shops and well-stocked supermarkets.

ONION, BOILING
Small, pungent onion, usually no more than 1 inch (2.5 cm) in diameter.

ONION, GREEN
Variety of onion harvested immature, leaves and all, before its bulb has formed. Green and white parts may both be enjoyed, raw or cooked, for their mild but still pronounced onion flavor. Also called spring onion or scallion.

ONION, RED
Mild, sweet variety of onion with purplish-red skin and red-tinged white flesh. Also known as Spanish onion.

ONION, YELLOW
Common, white-fleshed, strong-flavored onion distinguished by its dry, yellowish brown skin.

OREGANO
Aromatic, pungent and spicy Mediterranean herb—also known as wild marjoram—used fresh or dried as a seasoning for all kinds of savory dishes.

PAPRIKA
Powdered spice derived from the dried paprika pepper; popular in several European cuisines and available in sweet, mild and hot forms. Hungarian paprika is the best, but Spanish paprika, which is mild, may also be used.

PARMESAN
Hard, thick-crusted Italian cow's milk cheese with a sharp, salty, full flavor resulting from at least 2 years of aging. Buy in block form, to grate or shave fresh as needed. The finest of the many Italian varieties is designated parmigiano-reggiano.

PARSLEY
This popular fresh herb is available in two varieties: the more popular curly-leaf type and a flat-leaf type. The latter is also known as Italian parsley.

PEPPERCORNS
Pepper, the most common of all savory spices, is best purchased as whole peppercorns, to be ground in a pepper mill or coarsely crushed as needed. Pungent black peppercorns derive from slightly underripe pepper berries, whose hulls oxidize as they dry. Milder white peppercorns come from fully ripened berries, with the husks removed before drying. Sharp-tasting unripened green peppercorns are sold in water, pickled in brine or dried.

PINE NUTS
Small, ivory-colored seeds extracted from the cones of a species of pine tree, with a rich,

slightly resinous flavor. Used whole as an ingredient or garnish, or puréed as a thickener. Also known by the Italian *pinoli.*

PROSCIUTTO
Italian-style raw ham, a specialty of Parma, cured by dry-salting for 1 month, followed by air-drying in cool curing sheds for half a year or longer. Usually cut into tissue-thin slices.

RADICCHIO
Leaf vegetable related to **Belgian endive.** The most common variety has a spherical head, reddish purple leaves with creamy white ribs, and a mildly bitter flavor. Other varieties are slightly tapered and vary a bit in color. Served raw in salads, or cooked, usually by grilling. Also called red chicory.

RED PEPPER FLAKES
Coarsely ground flakes of dried red chilies, including seeds, which add moderately hot flavor to the foods they season.

REDUCE
To boil a liquid briskly until its volume decreases, thereby thickening its consistency and intensifying its flavor. A simple way to transform cooking liquid into a sauce.

RICE, ARBORIO
Popular Italian variety of rice with short, round grains high in starch content, which creates a creamy, saucelike consistency during cooking.

RICE, BROWN
Rice from which only the outer husk is removed during milling, leaving a highly nutritious, fiber-rich coating of bran that gives the grain its distinctive color, chewy texture and nutlike flavor.

ROMANO
Italian variety of cheese traditionally made from sheep's milk, now made from goat and cow's milk as well. Sold either fresh or, more commonly, aged. The aged form is similar to but notably more tangy than **Parmesan.** Buy in block form, to shave or grate as needed.

ROSEMARY
Mediterranean herb, used either fresh or dried, with a strong aromatic flavor well suited to lamb and veal, as well as poultry, seafood and vegetables.

SAFFRON
Intensely aromatic spice, golden orange in color, made from the dried stigmas of a species of crocus; used to perfume and color many classic Mediterranean and East Indian dishes. Sold either as threads—the dried stigmas—or in powdered form. Look for products labeled pure saffron.

SAGE
Pungent herb, used either fresh or dried, that goes particularly well with fresh or cured pork, lamb, veal or chicken.

SALT, SEA
Salt extracted by evaporation from sea water has a more pronounced flavor than regular table salt. Available in coarse and fine grinds in specialty-food stores and well-stocked supermarkets. Coarse or kosher salt may be used in place of coarse sea salt crystals.

STIR-FRY

A stove-top technique, Chinese in origin, for quickly cooking small pieces of food in a large pan over moderate to high heat.

To stir-fry chicken, first heat a Chinese wok or a large sauté pan over moderate to high heat. When the wok is hot, add just enough cooking oil to coat it lightly.

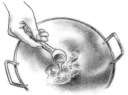

Add small, thin pieces of boneless, skinless chicken and stir and toss continuously for a few minutes, just until cooked through and very lightly golden.

Add vegetables, cut into small pieces, along with seasonings and a flavorful liquid such as chicken stock. Continue stirring until the vegetables are tender crisp and the liquid has reduced to a glaze.

SAUSAGE, MILD ITALIAN

Fresh Italian sausage is generally made from ground pork, seasoned with salt, pepper and spices. Those made in the style of northern Italy are usually sweet and mild, sometimes flavored with **fennel** seed. Southern-style sausages tend to be hotter, often flavored with flakes of dried chili pepper.

SHALLOT

Small member of the **onion** family with brown skin, white-to-purple flesh and a flavor resembling a cross between sweet onion and garlic.

SHERRY

Fortified, cask-aged wine, ranging in varieties from dry to sweet, enjoyed as an aperitif and used as a flavoring in both savory and sweet recipes.

SKIM

To remove impurities—whether scum or fat—from the surface of a liquid during cooking, thereby resulting in a clearer, cleaner-tasting final product. An essential early step in the preparation of chicken **stock.**

SOY SAUCE

Asian seasoning and condiment made from soybeans, wheat, salt and water. Seek out good-quality imported soy sauces.

STOCK

Flavorful liquid derived from slowly simmering chicken, meat, fish or vegetables in water, along with herbs and aromatic vegetables. Used as the primary cooking liquid in stews and braises, the foundation for sauces and soups, as well as a moist-ening and flavoring agent in other recipes. See chicken stock recipe on page 9.

TARRAGON

Fragrant, distinctively sweet herb used fresh or dried as a classic seasoning for chicken, light meats, seafood and eggs.

THYME

Fragrant, clean-tasting, small-leaved herb popular as a seasoning for poultry, light meats, seafood or vegetables. Used fresh or dried.

TOMATOES

During summer, when tomatoes are in season, use the best red, sun-ripened tomatoes you can find for cooking. At other times of year, plum tomatoes, sometimes called Roma or egg tomatoes, are likely to have the best flavor and texture.

TRUSS

To bind a chicken with heavy cotton or linen string to keep it compact, resulting in more even cooking and a more attractive presentation.

TURNIP

Small, creamy white root vegetable, tinged purple or green at its crown, with firm, pungent yet slightly sweet flesh. Generally cooked by boiling, braising or stewing. Choose smaller turnips that feel heavy for their size and are firm to the touch.

VERMOUTH

Dry or sweet wine commercially enhanced with herbs and barks to give it an aromatic flavor.

VINAIGRETTE

Classic French dressing or sauce for salad greens, vegetables, meats, poultry or seafood—literally "little vinegar." A combination of **vinegar** or some other acid such as lemon juice, seasonings and oil.

VINEGAR

Literally "sour" wine, vinegar results when certain strains of yeast cause wine—or some other alcoholic liquid—to ferment for a second time, turning it acidic. The best-quality wine vinegars begin with good-quality wine. Red wine vinegar, like the wine from which it is made, has a more robust flavor than vinegar produced from white wine. Balsamic vinegar, a specialty of Modena, Italy, is made from reduced grape juice aged for many years, taking on a rich, tart-sweet flavor; light, syrupy consistency and the deep purple color of a fine old wine.

WATERCRESS

Refreshing, slightly peppery, dark green leaf vegetable commercially cultivated and also found wild in freshwater streams. Used primarily in salads and as a popular garnish.

ZEST

Thin, brightly colored, outermost layer of a citrus fruit's peel, containing most of its aromatic essential oils—a lively source of flavor. Zest may be removed in one of three ways: with a simple tool known as a zester, drawn across the fruit's skin to remove the zest in thin strips; with a fine hand-held grater; or in wide strips with a vegetable peeler or a paring knife held almost parallel to the fruit's skin.

Index

ACKNOWLEDGMENTS

The publishers would like to thank the following people and organizations
for their generous assistance and support in producing this book:
George McWilliams, Amy Morton, Ken DellaPenta, Sharon-Ann C. Lott,
Stephen W. Griswold, the buyers for Gardener's Eden, and the buyers and
store managers for Pottery Barn and Williams-Sonoma stores.

The following kindly lent props for the photography: Biordi Art Imports,
Fillamento, Galisteo, Stephanie Greenleigh, Philippe Henry de Tessan,
Sue Fisher King, Karen Nicks, Lorraine & Judson Puckett,
Gianfranco Savio, Sue White and Chuck Williams.